SECRET CODES 2003

VOLUME 1

||||BRADYGAMES®
TAKE YOUR GAME FURTHER®

PlayStation® 2

THE GAMES

PlayStation® 2

L2   LI   R2   RI
D-Pad
Select   Start   X

AGGRESSIVE INLINE

Enter the following at the Cheats screen, which is found in the Options. The directions refer to the arrows below the alphabet.

All Characters

Enter the code Down, Right, Right, Down, Left, Down, Left, Down, Right, Right, Right.

All Levels, Park Editor Themes

Enter the code Up, Up, Down, Down, Left, Right, Left, Right, BABA.

All Keys

Enter the code **SKELETON**.

Invulnerable

Enter the code **KHUFU**.

Perfect Grind Balance

Enter the code **BIGUPYASELF**.

Perfect Handplant Balance

Enter the code **JUSTINBAILEY**.

Perfect Manual Balance

Enter the code **QUEZDONTSLEEP**.

Regenerating Juice

Enter the code Left, Left, Right, Right, Left, Right, Down, Up, Up, Down, AI.

Juice Remains After Crash

Enter the code BAKABAKA.

Better Wallrides

Enter the code Up, Down, Up, Down, Left, Right, Left, Right, ABABS.

Faster Spin

Enter the code Left, Left, Left, Left, Right, Right, Right, Right, Left, Right, Left, Right, Up.

BALDUR'S GATE DARK ALLIANCE

Level Warp and Invulnerability

Hold L1 + R2 + ▲ + Left and press START during gameplay.

Level 20 Character

Hold L1 + R2 + R3 + Left and press START during gameplay.

Gauntlet Mode

Complete the game.

Extreme Mode

Complete Gauntlet Mode.

Play as Drizzt

At the Main menu, hold L1 + R1 and press **X** + **▲**. Or, complete Extreme Mode.

BATMAN VENGEANCE

Enter the following codes at the Main menu.

All Cheats

Press L2, R2, L2, R2, ■, ■, ●, ●.

Unlimited Batcuffs

Press ■, ●, ■, ●, L2, R2, R2, L2.

Unlimited Bat Launcher

Press ●, ■, ●, ■, L1, R1, L2, R2.

Unlimited Electric Batarangs

Press L1, R1, L2, R2.

BLADE II

Main Menu Cheats

To turn these codes on and off, go to the Blade II logo menu screen.

Hold L1 and press the sequence of buttons. To turn off a cheat, reenter the same code. A message appears when the code has been successfully activated/deactivated.

Access All Missions

Press Down, Up, Left, Left, ●, Right, Down, ■.

Unlock All Weapons

Press ■, ●, Down, Left, ●, ●, ▲.

Unlock Daywalker Difficulty

Press Left, ●, Up, Down, ■, ●, **X**.

In-Game Cheats

To turn these cheats on and off, pause the game (press the START button).

Hold L1 and press the sequence of buttons. To turn off a cheat, reenter the same code. A message appears when the cheat has been successfully activated/deactivated.

Infinite Health

Press ▲, ■, ▲, ■, ▲, ●, ▲, ●.

Infinite Rage

Press Left, Down, Left, Down, Right, Up, Right, Up.

Friendlies Invulnerable

This cheat works in missions in which Blade must escort Whistler or Dr. Grant.

Press ■, ●, ▲, **X**, ■, ●, ▲, **X**.

Infinite Ammo

Press Left, ●, Right, ■, Up, ▲, Down, **X**.

CRASH BANDICOOT: THE WRATH OF CORTEX

Quick Time Trial in Wizards and Lizards

Pick up the clock and press the SELECT button. This teleports you to the end of the level.

DOWNFORCE

Invincibility

At the Main menu press L1, ▲, R1, ▲, Down, Down, ●.

Expert CPU

At the Main menu press ▲, Right, Left, ■, Up, ●, Down, Right.

Crash Arena

At the Main menu press Left, Right, Right, ■, Down, ▲, ▲, ■.

Crash Arena, 2-Player Mode

At the Main menu press Right, Left, Left, ●, Up, ▲, ▲, ■.

Beginner Trophy

At the Main menu press Right, Right, L1, ▲, ▲, R1, Right.

Intermediate Trophy

At the Main menu press Right (x2), ■, Left, L1, R1, ■ (x2).

Expert Trophy

At the Main menu press Right (x2), ●, Left, L1, ●, R1, ●.

Intermediate Championship

At the Main menu press Down, ■, Up, ■, Right (x2), Left.

Expert Championship

At the Main menu press Down, ●, Up, Down, ●, ●, R1, L1.

DROPSHIP: UNITED PEACE FORCE

Select Classified Files, press **X**, and enter the following codes:

Invincibility	TEAMBUDDIES
Unlimited Ammo	BLASTRADIUS
Level Select	KINGSLEY
Bonus Level 1	KREUZLER
Bonus Level 2	SHEARER
Bonus Level 3	UBERDOOPER

ENDGAME

Enter the following codes at the Main menu by firing the gun the specified number of times for each letter. This number represents the letter's numerical location in the alphabet. After each letter, reload and proceed to the next letter.

For example, for Arcade Mode you would enter BLAM. Or, fire the gun 2 times ("B"), reload, fire 12 times ("L"), reload fire I time ("A"), reload, then fire 13 times ("M"). The screen flashes when a code is correctly entered.

Master Code
Enter **MEBIGCHEAT**, or 13, 5, 2, 9, 7, 3, 8, 5, 1, 20.

Arcade Mode
Enter **BLAM**, or 2, 12, 1, 13. This becomes available in the Extras.

Country Challenges
Enter **ABROAD**, or 1, 2, 18, 15, 1, 4.

Mighty Joe Jupiter
Enter **MIGHTIER**, or 13, 9, 7, 8, 20, 9, 5, 18.

Music Test/Jukebox
Enter **LETSBOOGIE**, or 12, 5, 20, 19, 2, 15, 15, 7, 9, 5.

FREEKSTYLE

Select Enter Codes from the Options menu and enter the following:

All Characters, Outfits, Bikes, and Levels
Enter **LOKSMITH**.

All Characters
Enter **POPULATE**.

All Costumes
Enter **YARDSALE**.

All Bikes
Enter **WHEELS**.

All Tracks
Enter **TRAKMEET**.

Mike Jones
Enter **TOUGHGUY**.

Clifford Adoptante
Enter **COOLDUDE**.

Jessica Patterson
Enter **BLONDIE**.

Greg Albertyn
Enter **GIMEGREG**.

Unlimited Freekout
Enter **ALLFREEK**.

No Bike
Enter **FLYSOLO**.

Slow Motion
Enter **WTCHKPRS**.

Burn It Up Track
Enter **CARVEROK**.

Gnome Sweet Gnome Track
Enter **CLIPPERS**.

Let It Ride Track
Enter **BLACKJAK**.

Rocket Garden Track
Enter **TODAMOON**.

Crash Pad FreeStyle Track
Enter **WIDEOPEN**.

Burbs FreeStyle Track
Enter **TUCKELLE**.

Bikes

Enter the following codes to unlock more bikes.

Character	Bike	Code
Mike Metzger	Bloodshot	EYEDROPS
	Rock of Ages	BRRRRRAP
	Rhino Rage	SEVENTWO
Brian Deegan	Mulisha Man	WHATEVER
	Heavy Metal	HEDBANGR
	Dominator	WHOZASKN
Leeann Tweeden	Hot Stuff	OVENMITT
	Trendsetter	STYLIN
	Seducer	GOODLOOK
Stefy Bau	Amore	HEREIAM
	Disco Tech	SPARKLES
	211	TWONEONE
Clifford Adoptante	Gone Tiki	SUPDUDE
	Island Spirit	GOFLOBRO
	Hang Loose	STOKED
Mike Jones	Beater	KICKBUTT
	Lil' Demon	HORNS
	Flushed	PLUNGER

Character	Bike	Code
Jessica Patterson	Speedy	HEKACOOL
	Charged Up	LIGHTNIN
	Racer Girl	TONBOY
Greg Albertyn	The King	ALLSHOOK
	National Pride	PATRIOT
	Champion	NUMBE RI

Outfits

Enter the following codes to unlock more outfits.

Character	Outfit	Code
Mike Metzger	Ecko MX	HELLOOOO
	All Tatted Up	BODYART
Brian Deegan	Muscle Bound	RIPPED
	Commander	SOLDIER
Leeann Tweeden	Fun Lovin'	THNKPINK
	Red Hot	SPICY
Stefy Bau	Playing Jax	KIDSGAME
	UFO Racer	INVASION
Clifford Adoptante	Tiki	WINGS
	Tankin' It	NOSLEEVE
Mike Jones	Blue Collar	BABYBLUE
	High Roller	BOXCARS
Jessica Patterson	Warming Up	LAYERS
	Hoodie Style	NOT2GRLY
Greg Albertyn	Sharp Dresser	ILOOKGUD
	Star Rider	COMET

FREQUENCY

Before entering the following codes, press Down, Right, Up, Left, Left, Up, Right, Down at the Title screen.

Autocatcher in Solo

During gameplay press Left, Right, Right, Left, Up.

Multiplier in Solo

During gameplay press Right, Left, Left, Right, Up.

Bumper in Multi

During gameplay press Right, Left, Right, Left, Up.

Crippler in Multi

During gameplay press Left, Right, Left, Right, Down.

Freestyler in Multi

During gameplay press Left, Right, Right, Left, Down.

Neutralizer in Multi

During gameplay press Left, Right, Left, Right, Up.

Blur

During gameplay press Down, Up, Up, Down, Down, Up, Up, Down.

Gems Background

During gameplay press Up, Down, Up, Down, Left, Right, Right, Left.

No Track Boundary

During gameplay press Down, Up, Down, Up, Right, Left, Left, Right.

GIANTS: CITIZEN KABUTO

Cheat Menu

Enter **ALPUN** as a code.

Level Select

Enter **MBP4UJP** as a code.

Invincibility

Enter **MOLITOR** as a code.

Unlimited Ammo

Enter **FALLOUT** as a code.

Unlimited Jet Pack

Enter **38HK** as a code.

Unlimited Mana

Enter **BGDA** as a code.

Rainbow

Enter **DOROTHY** as a code.

Blue Screen

Enter **UDDOIT2** as a code.

Green Screen

Enter **SNIPEME** as a code.

Red Screen

Enter **ANGRY** as a code.

Zoom

Enter **CLOSEUP** as a code.

Front View

Enter **XTRASEE** as a code.

GODAI ELEMENTAL FORCE

Level Select

At the Main menu or during gameplay, press L1, L2, **X**, **▲**, L1, L2, **X**, **▲**.

Characters in Multiplayer

At the Main menu or during gameplay, press R2, **●**, **X**, **■**, **▲**, Right, Down, Left, Up, L2, L1, **●**, **■**, L1, L2, L1, **●**, L2, **■**.

Invincible Hiro

During gameplay press L1, L2, **●**, **■**, L1, L2, **●**, **■**.

I-Hit Kills for Hiro

During gameplay press L1, L2, Left Analog Stick Up, Left Analog Stick Down, Left Analog Stick Left, Left Analog Stick Right, **▲**, **■**, **X**, **●**.

All Magic

During gameplay press R1, R2, L1, L2, **X**, **▲**, **●**, **■**.

GRAND THEFT AUTO III

Better Vehicle Handling

Enter this code while outside your vehicle. This code makes all vehicles handle better. When activated, press L3 to make the car bounce.

Press R1, L1, R2, L1, Left, R1, R1, **▲**.

Vehicle Damage

Enter this code while inside the vehicle. Your car may look damaged, but it won't smoke and it returns to perfect condition.

Press R2, R2, L1, R1, Left, Down, Right, Up, Left, Down, Right, Up.

Explode All Vehicles

Press L2 R2 L1 R1 L2 R2 **▲** **■** **●** **▲** L2 L1.

Unlock the Rhino
Press ● (x6), R1, L2, L1, ▲, ●, ▲.

Invisible Car Chassis
Press L1, L1, ■, R2, ▲, L1, ▲.

Flying Vehicles
Press Right, R2, ●, R1, L2, Down, L1, R1.

Foggy
Press L1, L2, R1, R2, R2, R1, L2, **X**.

Cloudy
Press L1, L2, R1, R2, R2, R1, L2, ■.

Rain
Press L1, L2, R1, R2, R2, R1, L2, ●.

Normal Weather
Press L1, L2, R1, R2, R2, R1, L2, ▲.

Rioting Pedestrians
Press Down, Up, Left, Up, **X**, R1, R2, L2, L1.
NOTE: Once entered, this code CANNOT be reversed!

Pedestrians Out to Get You

Press Down, Up, Left, Up, **X**, R1, R2, L1, L2.
NOTE: Once entered, this code CANNOT be reversed!

Pedestrians Have Weapons

Press R2, R1, ▲, **X**, L2, L1, Up, Down.
NOTE: Once entered, this code CANNOT be reversed!

Increase Wanted Level

This increases the Wanted Level by two each time you enter it.
Press R2, R2, L1, R2, Left, Right, Left, Right, Left.

Wanted Level Down

This decreases the Wanted Level by two each time you enter it.
Press R2, R2, L1, R2, Up, Down, Up, Down, Up, Down.

Weapon Cheat

You can enter this code until you reach the maximum ammo amount (9999 for each weapon). When a weapon reaches its maximum ammo capacity, its ammunition supply becomes infinite.
Press R2, R2, L1, R2, Left, Down, Right, Up, Left, Down, Right, Up.

Change Character Model

NOTE: Once entered, this code CANNOT be reversed!
Press Right, Down, Left, Up, L1, L2, Up, Left, Down, Right.

Health Cheat

Press R2, R2, L1, R1, Left, Down, Right, Up, Left, Down, Right, Up.

Armor Cheat

Press R2, R2, L1, L2, Left, Down, Right, Up, Left, Down, Right, Up.

Money Cheat

Press R2, R2, L1, L1, Left, Down, Right, Up, Left, Down, Right, Up.

Increase the Gore

Press ■, L1, ●, Down, L1, R1, ▲, Right, L1, ✕.

Slower Gameplay

You can enter this code three times for even slower gameplay. Press ▲, Up, Right, Down, ■, R1, R2.

Faster Gameplay

You can enter this code three times for even faster gameplay. Press ▲, Up, Right, Down, ■, L1, L2.

Speed Up Time

Press ● (x3), ■ (x5), L1, ▲, ●, ▲.
NOTE: You can enter this code a second time to return to normal time.

GRAN TURISMO 3 A-SPEC

Professional Difficulty

Select Arcade Mode, then choose Single Race. At the Level Select screen highlight Hard, hold L1 + R1 and select it for Pro Level.

GRAVITY GAMES BIKE: STREET. VERT. DIRT

Select Cheat Code from the Options menu and enter the following:

Unlock Everything
Enter **LOTACRAP**.

All Bikes
Enter **PIKARIDE**.

Bird Brains
Enter **FLYAWAY**.

Angus Sigmund
Enter **SIGMAN**.

Bobby Bones
Enter **BONEGUY**.

Pierce
Enter **BADGIRL**.

Max Stats
Enter **MAXSTATS**.

Ramp Granny
Enter **OLDLADY**.

Dennis McCoy Max Stats
Enter **DMCDMAN**.

Oil Refinery
  Enter **OILSPILL**.

Train Depot
  Enter **CHOOCHOO**.

Mount Magma
  Enter **VOLCANO**.

Museum District
  Enter **ARTRIDER**.

Gravity Games Street
  Enter **PAVEMENT**.

Museum District Competition
  Enter **ARTCOMP**.

Gravity Games Vert
  Enter **GGFLYER**.

Fuzzy's Yard
  Enter **FUZYDIRT**.

Gravity Games Dirt
  Enter **MUDPUDLE**.

Andre Ellison's Movie
  Enter **ANDFMV**.

Dennis McCoy's Movie
  Enter **DMCFMV**.

Leigh Ramsdell's Movie
  Enter **LEIFMV**.

Fuzzy Hall's Movie
  Enter **FUZFMV**.

Mat Berringer's Movie
  Enter **MATFMV**.

Jamie Bestwick's Movie
  Enter **JAMFMV**.

Reuel Erikson's Movie
  Enter **REUFMV**.

GUILTY GEAR X

Testament and Dizzy

At the Title screen press Down, Right, Right, Up, START.

HERDY GERDY

Cheat Mode

At the Title screen press L2, L1, L2, L1, Up, R1, R2, R1, R2, Down, SELECT.

HIDDEN INVASION

Easy Cheat

At the Title screen press Up, Down, Down, Up, Left, Left, Up, Right, Right, Up, Up, Up.

Big Heads

At the Title screen press Left, Left, Up, Up, Right, Right, Down, Down.

HIGH HEAT MAJOR LEAGUE BASEBALL 2003

Cheat Mode

Pause the game and press ■, ■, ●, ●, L1, R1. Then press L1 + L2 + R1 + R2.

KELLY SLATER'S PRO SURFER

Select Cheats from the Extras menu and enter the following cell phone numbers. Turn them on and off by selecting Toggle Cheat.

Max Stats
Enter 2125551776.

High Jump
Enter 2175550217.

Perfect Balance
Enter 2135555721.

1st-Person View
Enter 8775553825. Select Camera Settings from the Options menu.

Trippy
Enter 8185551447.

Mega Cheat
Enter 7145558092.

All Levels
Enter **3285554497**.

All Suits
Enter **7025552918**.

All Surfers
Enter **9495556799**.

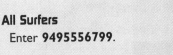

All Tricks
Enter **6265556043**.

Surfers

Surfer	Cell Number
Freak	3105556217

Surfer	Cell Number
Tiki God	8885554506

Surfer	Cell Number
Tony Hawk	3235559787

Surfer	Cell Number
Travis Pastrana	8005556292

LEGACY OF KAIN: BLOOD OMEN 2

Begin Game with Soul Reaver and Iron Armor

At the Main menu press L1, R1, L2, R2, ■, ●, ▲.

Refill Blood

Press L2 to access the map screen, then press Up, Right, ■, ●, Up, Down, Right, Left.

Refill Magic

Press L2 to access the map screen, then press Right (x2), ■, ●, Up, Down, Right, Left.

Extra Movie

At the Main menu press Up, Up, Down, Right, Left.

LEGACY OF KAIN: SOUL REAVER 2

All Bonus Materials

At the Main menu press Left, ▲, Right, ▲, Down, ●, **X**.

LEGENDS OF WRESTLING

All Wrestlers

At the Main menu press Up, Up, Down, Down, Left, Right, Left, Right, ▲, ▲, ■.

LOTUS CHALLENGE

All Cars and Courses

Enter **CRAIGSAYS** as the driver name.

MAT HOFFMAN'S PRO BMX 2

Level Select

At the Title screen press ■, Right, Right, ▲, Down, ■. This works for Session, Free Ride, and Multiplayer modes.

Boston, MA Level (Road Trip)

At the Title screen press ■, Up, Down, Down, Up, ■.

Chicago, IL Level (Road Trip)

At the Title screen press ■, Up, ▲, Up, ▲, ■.

Las Vegas, NV Level (Road Trip)

At the Title screen press ■, R1, Left, L1, Right, ■.

Los Angeles, CA Level (Road Trip)

At the Title screen press ■, Left, ▲, ▲, Left, ■.

New Orleans, LA Level (Road Trip)

At the Title screen press ■, Down, Right, Up, Left, ■.

Portland, OR Level (Road Trip)

At the Title screen press ■, X, X, ▲, ▲, ■.

Day Smith

At the Title screen press ▲, Up, Down, Up, Down, ■.

Vanessa

At the Title screen press ▲, Down, Left, Left, Down, ■.

Big Foot

At the Title screen press ▲, Right, Up, Right, Up, ■.

The Mime
At the Title screen press ▲, Left, Right, Left, Right, Left.

Volcano
At the Title screen press ▲, Up, Up, **X**, Up, Up, **X**.

Elvis Costume
At the Title screen press ●, L1, L1, Up, Up.

BMX Costume
At the Title screen press ●, ▲, Left, Right, Left, ●.

Tiki Battle Mode
At the Title screen press L1, L1, Down, R1, **X**, L1.

Mat Hoffman Videos

At the Title screen press R1, Left, ●, Left, ●, Left, R1.

Joe Kowalski Videos

At the Title screen press R1, Up, **X**, **▲**, Down, R1.

Rick Thorne Videos

At the Title screen press R1, L1, Right, R1, Left, R1.

Mike Escamilla Videos

At the Title screen press R1, ●, **X**, **X**, ●, **X**, **X**, R1.

Simon Tabron Videos

At the Title screen press R1, L1, L1, R1, L1, L1, R1.

Kevin Robinson Videos

At the Title screen press R1, **X**, **▲**, Down, Up, R1.

Cory Nastazio Videos

At the Title screen press R1, ■, ●, ●, ■ (x3), R1.

Ruben Alcantara Videos

At the Title screen press R1, Left, Right, Left, Right, Left, Right, R1.

Seth Kimbrough Videos

At the Title screen press R1, Up, Up, ● (x3), R1.

Nate Wessel Videos

At the Title screen press R1, Down, **▲**, ●, Down, **▲**, ●, R1.

Big Ramp Video

At the Title screen press R1, Up, Down, Left, **X**, **X**, **X**, R1.

Day Flatland Video
At the Title screen press R1, ●, Left, Left, ■, Right, Right, R1.

All Music
At the Title screen press L1, Left, Left, Right (x3), **X, X**.

MAX PAYNE

All Weapons & Full Ammo
Pause the game and press L1, L2, R1, R2, ▲, ●, **X**, ■.

Unlimited Health
Pause the game and press L1, L1, L2, L2, R1, R1, R2, R2.

Level Select
Play through the first chapter of the Subway. Then at the Main menu press Up, Down, Left, Right, Up, Left, Down, ●. Now go to Load Level and choose a destination.

Slow Motion Sounds
Enter this code at the Pause screen.
Press L1, L2, R1, R2, ▲, ■, **X**, ●.

Unlimited Bullet Time
Enter this code at the Pause screen.
Press L1, L2, R1, R2, ▲, **X**, **X**, ▲.

MEDAL OF HONOR FRONTLINE

Select Passwords from the Options menu and enter the following. You need to turn on many of these cheats at the Bonus screen.

Gold Stars in All Missions/All Bonuses
Enter **DAWOIKS**.

Mission Skip
After turning on this cheat, the current mission will be complete with a Gold Star.

Enter **MONKEY**.

I-Hit Kills
Enter **WHATYOUGET**.

Invisible Enemy Cheat
Enter **WHERERU**.

Rubber Grenades
Enter **BOING**.

MOHton Torpedo
Enter **TPDOMOHTON**.

Snipe-o-Rama
Enter **LONGSHOT**.

Perfectionist
Enter **URTHEMAN**.

Achilles Head
Enter **GLASSIAW**.

Invincible

Pause the game and press ■, L1, ●, R1, ▲, L2, SELECT, R2.

Unlimited Ammo

Pause the game and press ●, L2, ■, L1, SELECT, R2, ▲, SELECT.

A Storm in the Port Mission
Enter **ORANGUTAN**.

Horten's Nest Mission
Enter **GORILLA**.

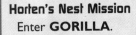

Several Bridges Too Far Mission
Enter **CHIMPNZEE**.

Rolling Thunder Mission
Enter **LEMUR**.

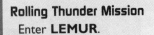

Making of D-Day
Enter **BACKSTAGEO**

Making of Needle in a Haystack
Enter **BACKSTAGER**.

Making of Horten's Nest
Enter **BACKSTAGES**.

Making of Several Bridges Too Far
Enter **BACKSTAGEF**.

Men with Hats
Enter **HABRDASHR**.

MEN IN BLACK 2: ALIEN ESCAPE

Invincible

At the Title screen press Right, **X**, R1, **▲**, Up, L2, **X**, Left, L1, **●**, **X**, R2.

All Weapons

At the Title screen press Up, Down, **X**, **■**, R1, **▲**, **▲**, Left, **●**, L1, L1, Right.

Level Select

At the Title screen press R2, **▲**, Left, **●**, **■**, L2, Left, Up, **X**, Down, L2, **■**.

Training Missions

At the Title screen press **■**, Up, L2, Left, **▲**, **X**, R2, **●**, Right, R1, **■**, **●**.

Boss Mode

At the Title screen press R1, **▲**, Down, Down, **X**, L2, Left, **■**, Right, **▲**, R2, L1.

No Power-Up Drops

At the Title screen press Down, Up, **X**, **■**, Down, Up, **X**, **■**, L1, L2, **■**, **●**.

Full Area Effect

At the Title screen press Left, **X**, **▲**, Up, **X**, Down, **■**, L2, Left, R2.

Full Beam

At the Title screen press Left, **●**, **▲**, Right, L1, **■**, Left, R1, R1, **▲**.

Full Bolt

At the Title screen press Left, Right, Up, Down, L1, **●**, **▲**, R2, Left, Down, **■**, **■**.

Full Homing

At the Title screen press Right, Up, ■, L1, Left, Left, L1, Left, ●, Left.

Full Spread

Press L2, R1, ●, L2, Down, Up, L1, Right, Left, **X**.

Agent Data

At the Title screen press Up, Down, ●, R2, Left, L2, Right, **X**, R2, ■, Up, R1.

Alien Data

At the Title screen press ■, L1, ●, L2, Down, ▲, R1, Right, **X**, Left, R2, ▲.

Making Of Video

Press ●, R2, L2, ●, ▲, Down, ■, **X**, Right, L1, **X**, Up.

MIKE TYSON
HEAVYWEIGHT BOXING

Platinum Unlock

At the Title screen press ■, ●, L2, R2. This unlocks all Modes, all Boxers, and all Arenas.

Big Head Mode
At the Title screen press ■, ●, Up, Down.

Small Head Mode
At the Title screen press ■, ●, Down, Up.

2-D Mode
At the Title screen press
Down, Up, ●, ■.

Super Mutant Mode
At the Title screen press ■, Left, Up, ▲.

Custom Boxer Textures
At the Title screen press LI, RI, **X**, **X**, ▲, **X**.

Unlock Codies Credits
At the Title screen press **X**, ▲, ■, ●.

MISTER MOSQUITO

Kaneyo Mosquito
At the Character Select
screen, press and hold LI and
press Up, Right, Left, Down,
■, ■, RI, RI, RI.

Kenichi Mosquito
After entering the Kaneyo Mosquito code, hold L2 and
press Up, Right, Left, Down, ■, ■, R2, R2, R2 at the
Character Select screen.

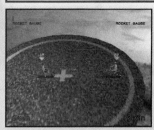

2-Player Mini Game

Turn on the system and hold START + SELECT on controller two.

MLB SLUGFEST 20-03

Cheats

At the Match-Up screen, use ■, ▲ and ● to enter the following codes, then press the appropriate direction. For example, for Rubber Ball press ■ two times, ▲ four times, ● two times, then press Up.

Tournament Mode
111 Down

Big Head
200 Right

Unlimited Turbo
444 Down

Max Power
030 Left

No Fatigue
343 Up

Max Speed
003 Left

Max Batting
300 Left

Log Bat
004 Up

Mace Bat
004 Left

Wiffle Bat
004 Right

Rubber Ball
242 Up

Roman Coliseum
333 Up

Pinto Team
210 Right

Eagle Team
212 Right

Todd McFarlane Team
222 Right

Tiny Head
200 Left

Extra Time After Plays
123 Up

16" Softball
242 Down

Rocket Park Stadium
321 Up

Horse Team
211 Right

Lion Team
220 Right

Team Terry Fitzgerald
333 Right

NASCAR HEAT 2002

Challenge Skip in Beat the Heat

At the Main menu press Up, Down, Left, Right, R1, Right, Left.

Arcade Style Beat the Heat Mode

At the Main menu press Up, Down, Left, Right, R1, Left, Right.

Hardcore Realism Mode

At the Main menu press Up, Down, Left, Right, R1, Up, Down.

Clean Screen During Replay

At the Main menu press Up, Down, Left, Right, R1, Down, Up. Press ● during the replay.

Shoot Tires

In Single Race or Head-to-Head mode, enter the following cheats at the Race Day screen. Press Up to fire.

Code	Enter
Shoot Balls in race	Up, Down, Left, Right, R1, Up, Up
Shoot Balls in practice	Up, Down, Left, Right, R1, Down, Down

NASCAR THUNDER 2002

Extra Cars

Select Create-a-Car and enter the name as the following:

Audrey Clark	Kristi Jones
Rick Edwards	Joey Joulwan
Michelle Emser	Dave Alpern
Katrina Goode	Buster Auton
Diane Grubb	Scott Brewer
Jim Hannigan	Cheryl King
Troi Hayes	Mandy Misiak
Crissy Hillsworth	Josh Neelon
Traci Hultzapple	Dave Nichols
Rick Humphrey	

Benny Parsons

Ken Patterson
Dick Paysor
Tom Renedo
Sasha Soares
Chuck Spicer
Daryl Wolfe

NASCAR THUNDER 2003

Fantasy Drivers

Create a car with the name Extra Drivers.

Dale Earnhardt

Create a car with the name Dale Earnhardt.

NCAA GAMEBREAKER 2003

Stadium Easter Eggs

Stadium	Enter
Bayside Park Stadium	FOGGY
Coliseum Stadium (Alt)	MAXIMVS
CVN-99 Stadium	FLATTOP
Desert Stadium	TUMBLEWEED
Easter Egg Island Stadium (Alt)	LAVA
Easter Egg Island Stadium (Alt)	SNEAKYTIKI
Emerald Stadium	GRUNGE
Hanger Stadium	UFO
High Bluff Stadium	HACIENDA
I-989 Stadium	INTERSTATE
Space Station Redzone Stadium (Alt)	TOBOR
Space Station Redzone Stadium	ALPHA
Temple of Apep Stadium (Alt)	FANG
Temple of Apep stadium	COBRA

NEED FOR SPEED: HOT PURSUIT 2

Unlock HSV Coupe GTS

At the Main menu press L1, L2, L1, L2, R1, ▲, R1, ▲.

Unlock BMW Z8

At the Main menu press ■,
Right, ■, Right, R2, ▲, R2, ▲.

Unlock Porsche Carerra GT

At the Main menu press Left, Right, Left, Right, R1, R2, R1, R2.

Unlock Ferrari F550

At the Main menu press L1, ■, L1, ■, Right, R1, Right, R1.

Unlock Ferrari F50

At the Main menu press L1, ▲, L1, ▲, Right, L2, Right, L2.

Unlock McLaren F1 LM

At the Main menu press ■, L1, ■, L1, ▲, Right, ▲, Right.

NFL BLITZ 20-03

Cheats

Use L2, R2 and **X** to enter the following codes, then press the specified direction. For example, for Super Field Goals press L2 once, R2 twice, **X** three times, then press Left.

Code	Enter
Tournament Mode	111 Down
More Time to Enter Codes	212 Right
Extra Time	001 Right
Show More Field	021 Right
Auto Icon Passing	003 Up
No Auto Icon Passing	003 Down
Extra Play for Offense	333 Down
Smart CPU Teammates	314 Down
Always QB, 2 Humans/Team	222 Left

Always Receiver, 2 Humans/Team	222 Right
No First Downs	210 Up
No Highlight, Target Player	321 Down
No Interceptions	355 Up
No Punting	141 Up
No Random Fumbles	523 Down
No Replays	554 Right
No CPU Assist	012 Down
Allow Stepping Out of Bounds	211 Left
Butter Fingers	345 Up
Infinite Turbo	415 Up
Faster Running Speed	032 Left
Fast Passes	240 Left
Super Blitzing	054 Up
Super Field Goals	123 Left

Power-Up Offense	412 Up
Power-Up Defense	421 Up
Power-Up Linemen	521 Up
Big Heads	200 Right

Big Head Teams	203 Right
Huge Heads	145 Left
Big Feet	025 Left
Power Loader	025 Right

Code	Enter
Chimp Mode	025 Up

Noftle Mode	325 Up
Showtime Mode	351 Right
Weather: Snow	555 Left
Weather: Rain	555 Right
Clear Weather	123 Right
Ground Fog	232 Down
Chrome Ball	030 Down
Classic Ball	030 Left
Arctic Station	034 Down

Central Park	033 Right

Training Grounds	035 Up
Team: Armageddon	543 Right

Code	Enter
Team: Bilders	310 Up

Code	Enter
Team: Brew Dawgs	432 Down
Team: Crunch Mode	403 Right
Team: Gsmers	501 Up
Team: Midway	253 Right
Team: Neo Tokyo	344 Down

Code	Enter
Team: Rollos	254 Up

Hidden Players

Enter the following ID and PIN to play as that character:

ID	PIN
BEAR	1985
CLOWN	1974

ID	PIN
COWBOY	1996
DEER	1997

ID	PIN
DOLPHIN	1972
EAGLE	1981

ID	PIN
HORSE	1999
PATRIOT	2002

ID	PIN
LION	1963
PINTO	1966

ID	PIN
PIRATE	2001
RAM	2000

ID	PIN
TIGER	1977
VIKING	1977

NO ONE LIVES FOREVER

Mission Select

Highlight Load Game at the Main menu. Then press and hold L3 + R3 and press **X**.

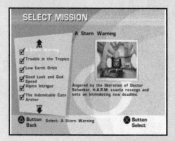

PROJECT EDEN

Cheats

During gameplay, press **X** to access the team screen. Rotate the Left Analog Stick clockwise three times and then counter-clockwise three times. A new icon should appear in the lower-right corner of the screen. Select it for the following cheats:

Max Energy

Turn On Invulnerability

Turn On Team Invulnerability

Turn Off Team Invulnerability

Turn On Infinite Weapon Energy

All Weapons

Access All Levels

Skip Level

RAYMAN ARENA

After entering one of the names listed here, press L2 + ● + ■ to enter it.

All Characters
Enter **PUPPETS**.

All Skins
Enter **CARNIVAL**.

All Levels
Enter **ALLRAYMANM**.

All Battle Levels
Enter **ALLFISH**.

All Race Levels
Enter **ALLTRIBES**.

Old TV Screen
Enter **OLDTV**.

SAVAGE SKIES

Complete All Objectives
Pause the game and press Left, Right, Right, Down, Up, Down, Down, **X**.

All Multi-Player Levels
At the Main menu press Left, Right, Left, Right, Up, Left, Right, **X**.

Invincibility
Pause the game and press Left, Left, Right, Right, Up, Up, **X**.

All Creatures
At the Main menu press Left, Right, Left, Left, Right, **X**.

Crystal
Pause the game and press Left, Right, Left, Up, Right, Down, Left, **X**, **X**.

SCOOBY DOO: NIGHT OF 100 FRIGHTS

All Power-ups

Pause the game, hold L1 + L2 + R1 + R2 and press ●, ■, ●, ■, ●, ■ (x3), ●, ●, ■, ● (x3).

Movie Gallery

Pause the game, hold L1 + L2 + R1 + R2 and press ■ (x3), ● (x3), ■, ●, ■.

Alternate Credits

Pause the game, hold L1 + L2 + R1 + R2 and press ■, ●, ●, ■, ●, ■.

Holidays

Change the system date to one of the following dates to change the appearance slightly:

January 1
July 4
October 31
December 25

SKYGUNNER

Variable/Uniform Processing

When unlocked, this is located in the Configuration Menu.

At the Title screen press Up, ▲, Left, ●, Down, X, Right, ■.

Unlock Everything

At the Title screen hold L1+R1 and press ●, ■, Up, ●, ▲, Down.

SLED STORM

All Characters

At the Title screen press and hold L1+R1 and press ●, ▲, ●, ▲, ●, Down.

All Sleds

At the Title screen press and hold L1+R1 and press ●, ■, ●, ■, ●, Left.

All Tracks

At the Title screen press and hold L1+R1 and press ●, Left, ●, Right, ●, Up.

Hover Sled

At the Title screen press and hold L1+R1 and press ●, ▲, ■, ●, ▲, Right.

SMUGGLER'S RUN 2: HOSTILE TERRITORY

Level Select and All Cars

Pause the game and press L2, R2, R2, L2, R1, L2, L1, Left, Right, L2, Down, R2.

Invisibility

Pause the game and press R1, L1, L1, R2, L1, L1, L2.

Light Cars

Pause the game and press L1, R1, R1, L2, R2, R2.

No Gravity

Pause the game and press R1, R2, R1, R2, Up (x3).

Slower Speed

You can enter this code up to three times.

Pause the game and press R2, L2, L1, R1, Left (x3).

Faster Speed

You can enter this code up to three times.

Pause the game and press R1, L1, L2, R2, Right (x3).

SPIDER-MAN: THE MOVIE

Unlock Everything
Enter ARACHNID.

Small Character
  Enter **SPIDERBYTE**.

Big Head & Feet
  Enter **GOESTOYOURHEAD**.

Big Head Enemies
  Enter **JOELSPEANUTS**.

Goblin-Style Costume
  Enter **FREAKOUT**.

Mary Jane
  Enter **GIRLNEXTDOOR**.

Scientist
  Enter **SERUM**.

Police Officer
  Enter **REALHERO**.

Captain Stacey
  Enter **CAPTAINSTACEY**.

The Shocker
  Enter **HERMANSCHULTZ**.

Thug 1
  Enter **KNUCKLES**.

Thug 2
  Enter **STICKYRICE**.

Thug 3
  Enter **THUGSRUS**.

Unlimited Webbing
  Enter **ORGANICWEBBING**.

All Combat Controls
  Enter **KOALA**.

Extra-Cool Attacks
  Enter **DODGETHIS**.

Super Coolant
  Enter **CHILLOUT**.

Level Select
  Enter **IMIARMAS**.

Level Skip
  Enter **ROMITAS**. Pause the game and select Next Level to advance.

Pinhead Bowling Training Level
  Enter **HEADEXPLODY**.

1st-Person View
  Enter **UNDERTHEMASK**.

STAR WARS: RACER REVENGE

Before entering the following codes, set a record and enter your name as **NO TIME**.

Hard Mode

At the Main menu, hold L1 + L2 + R1 + R2 and press ▲.

All Tracks

At the Main menu, hold L1 + L2 + R1 + R2 and press Right, Left, Right, Left, ●, ■, ●, ■.

Art Galleries

At the Main menu, hold L1 + L2 + R1 + R2 and press Right, ■, Left, ●, Down, **X**, Up, ▲.

STATE OF EMERGENCY

Invulnerability

During gameplay, press L1, L2, R1, R2, **X**.

Unlimited Ammo

During gameplay, press L1, L2, R1, R2, **▲**.

Mission Skip

During gameplay, press Left, Left, Left, Left, **▲**.

Infinite Time in Chaos Mode

During gameplay, press L1, L2, R1, R2, **●**.

Little Player

During gameplay, press R1, R2, L1, L2, **X**.

Big Player

During gameplay, press R1, R2, L1, L2, **▲**.

Normal Player

During gameplay, press R1, R2, L1, L2, ●.

Punches Decapitate

During gameplay, press L1, L2, R1, R2, ■.

Increase Looting

During gameplay, press R1, L1, R2, L2, ▲.

Bull

During gameplay, press Right (x4), **X**.

Freak

During gameplay, press Right (x4), ●.

Spanky

During gameplay, press Right (x4), ▲.

STREET HOOPS

Select Cheats from Game Settings and enter the following:

Kung Fu

Press ●, ●, ■, L1.

Tuxedo

Press L2, L2, ●, ■.

I Heart NY Uniforms
Press ●, L1, ●, ■, R2, L1, L2, L1.

Elvis Uniforms
Press R1, L1, R1, L1, R2, L1, L2, L1.

Lederhosen Uniforms
Press ■, R1, R1, R1, R2, L1, L2, L1.

Brick City Clothing
Press ■, R1, R2, ●, ●, ●, ■, ●.

And I Ball

Press R1, ●, ■, ■, L1, ●, ●, R2.

Globe Ball

Press R1, L1, L2, ●, L1, ●, ●, R2.

Court Select Ball

Press ●, L1, R2, ●, L1, ●, ●, R2.

Black Ball

Press R2, R2, ●, L2.

Easier Steals

Press ■, R2, ■, R1, ●, L1, ●, L2.

Easier Blocks

Press R1, ●, L2, R2.

STUNTMAN

Select New Game and enter the following as a name. You should get a confirmation when entered correctly.

All Driving Games, Cars, and Toys
Enter **Bindl**.

All Cars
Enter **spiDER**.

All Toys
Enter **MeFf**.

SUPERMAN: SHADOW OF APOKOLIPS

Select Cheat Codes from the Options menu and enter the following:

Expert Mode
Enter **BIZZARO**.

Unlimited Health
Enter **SMALLVILLE**.

Unlimited Superpowers
Enter **JOR EL**.

All Movies
Enter **LANA LANG**.

All Biographies
Enter **LARA**.

TEKKEN 4

Panda
Highlight Kuma and press ● or ▲.

Violet
Highlight Lee and press ●.

TEST DRIVE

Unlock Everything
At the Main menu press Right, Right, Left, ■, Up, L2, L2,

R I.SoundMAX and SPX Cars

Unlock all of the cars and enter the San Francisco Drag Race. Select the Dodge Concept Viper and set a time record, then enter SOUNDMAX as a name.

THE MARK OF KRI

Enter the following codes at the Title screen. Then during gameplay, visit the Sage in the back of the Inn to turn on the cheats.

Arena Enemies AI

Press **X**, ● (x3), **X**, ■ (x3), **X**, ●, ■, **X**.

Tougher Enemies

Press **X**, ●, ■, ■, **X**, ■, ●, ●, **X**, ●, ●, **X**.

Unlimited Arrows

Press **X, ●, ■, ■, X, ■, ●, ●, X, ■, ■, X**.

Weaker Enemies

Press **X, ●, ●, ■, X, ■, ■, ●**.

Full Health Power

Press **X** (x4), **■** (x4), **●** (x4).

Invincible Rau

Press **■, ●, X, ■, ●, ■, X, ●, X, ■, ●, X**.

TONY HAWK'S PRO SKATER 3

All Cheats

Select Cheats from the Options menu and enter backdoor. You can access the cheats from the Pause menu.

All Movies

Select Cheats from the Options menu and enter **Peepshow**.

Complete Game

Select Cheats from the Options menu and enter **ROAD-TRIP**.

All Characters

Select Cheats from the Options menu and enter **YOHOMIES**.

Max Stats

Select Cheats from the Options menu and enter **PUMP-MEUP**.

TRANSWORLD SURF

Enter the following cheats during a game in Pro Tour Mode.

Enable Cheats

Enter **SELECT**, Up, Down, L2, Left, Right, L2.

Complete All Goals

Enter **SELECT**, Up, Left, L1, Up, Left, L1.

Max Out Trick Meter

Enter **SELECT**, Up, Down, Left, Right, Down, Up.

Fast Paddle

Enter **SELECT**, Up, Down, Left, Right, Down, Down.

Perfect Floater Balance

Enter **SELECT**, Up, Down, Left, Right, Right, Left.

Invisible

Enter **SELECT**, Up, Down, Left, Right, Left, Up.

Invisible Surfboard

Enter **SELECT**, Up, Down, Left, Right, Left, Down.

Surf on a shark

Enter **SELECT**, Up, Down, Left, Right, Right, Down.

All Levels

Enter **SELECT**, Down, Right, Left, L1, Down, Right, Left, L1.

Toggle HUD

Enter **SELECT**, Up, Down, Left, Right, Up, Right.

Free Floating Camera

Enter **SELECT**, Right, Left, Down, Up, L1. This can only be done in Free Surf Mode. Use the Analog Sticks to move the camera.

Disable Cheats

Enter **SELECT**, **SELECT**, **SELECT**, **SELECT**.

TUROK: EVOLUTION

Select Enter Cheats from the Cheats menu and enter the following:

All Cheats

Enter **FMNFB**.

Invincible

Enter **EMERPUS**.

All Weapons

Only applies to weapons available in that level.

Enter **TEXAS**.

Unlimited Ammo

Enter **MADMAN**.

Level Select

Enter **SELLOUT**.

Invisibility

Enter **SLLEWGH**.

Big Heads

Enter **HEID**.

Zoo Mode

Enter **ZOO**.

Demo Mode/Mini Game

Enter **HUNTER**.

TWISTED METAL: BLACK

Set the Control option to Classic to enter the following codes. You must enter these codes during gameplay.

Turn Weapons Into Health

Press and hold L1 + R1 + L2 + R2 and press ▲, **X**, ■, ●.

Infinite Ammo

Press and hold L1 + R1 + L2 + R2 and press Up, **X**, Left, ●.

Invulnerability

Press and hold L1 + R1 + L2 + R2 and press Right, Left, Down, Up.

God Mode

Press and hold L1 + R1 + L2 + R2 and press Up, **X**, Left, ●.

Mega Guns

Press and hold L1 + R1 + L2 + R2 and press **X**, **X**, ▲.

Killer Weapons & 1-Hit Kills

Press and hold L1 + R1 + L2 + R2 and press **X**, **X**, Up. Re-enter the code to disable it.

Enhanced Freeze Attack

Press and hold L1 + R1 + L2 + R2 and press Right, Left, Up.

WAY OF THE SAMURAI

Full Health

Pause the game, hold L1 + L2 and press Down, Up, Down, Up, Right, Left, ●.

All Sword Skills

Select Versus Mode and pause the game. Then hold R1 and press R2, R2, L1, L1, L2, L2. Release R1 and press R2.

Random Sword

At the Sword Inventory screen, hold L1 + R1 and press ●, Down, Down, Up, Up, Down, Up, ●.

Change Characters

At the New Game screen, press L1, R1, R1, L2 (x3), R2, R2, R2 + ■. Press Left or Right to choose a character.

Battle Mode

At the Title screen, hold L1 + R1 and press ● + ■.

Increase Sword Durability

Pause the game, hold R1 + R2, and press Right, Right, Left, Left, Down, Up, ●.

WIPEOUT FUSION

Select Cheats from the Extras menu and enter the following:

Features Unlocked

Enter **X, ▲, ●, ▲, ●**.

Infinite Shields

Enter **▲, ▲, ■, ■, ■**.

Infinite Weapons

Enter **▲, ●, X, ●, ■**.

Animal Ships

Enter **▲, ●, ●, ▲, X**.

Super Fast Ships

Enter **■, X, X, X, ▲**.

Mini-Ships

Enter **●, ■, ■, X, ●**.

Retro Planes

Enter **X, ●, ▲, ■, X**.

THE GAMES

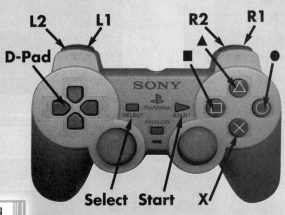

007 RACING

All Cheats

Select Mission Mode and enter your name as MMMQRRQ.

102 DALMATIANS: PUPPIES TO THE RESCUE

Passwords

Level	Password
2	Dice, Bone, Bone, Dice
3	Dice, Key, Bone, Machine
4	Dice, Bone, Food Bowl, Toy
5	Bone, Dice, Dog, Bone
6	Bone, Dice, Machine, Food Bowl
7	Bone, Bone, Paw, Dog
8	Bone, Bone, Paw, Toy
9	Bone, Toy, Key, Bone
10	Bone, Toy, Key, Dice
11	Bone, Toy, Bone, Machine
12	Bone, Machine, Dice, Toy
13	Bone, Machine, Toy, Key
14	Bone, Toy, Paw, Food Bowl
15	Bone, Toy, Toy, Machine
16	Bone, Paw, Toy, Toy
17	Toy, Bone, Key, Bone
Bonus 1	Machine, Dice, Dice, Dice
Bonus 2	Machine, Dice, Dice, Machine

ACTION MAN: MISSION XTREME

All Tools and Weapons

Pause the game and press L1, L2, R2.

Invincibility

Pause the game and press L1, R2, R1.

ARMY MEN: WORLD WAR FINAL FRONT

All Weapons

Pause the game, hold R1 + L2, and press **X** ,**●**, Up, Up, **■**, Down.

C-12: FINAL RESISTANCE

Invincible

Pause the game, hold L2, and press Up, Left, Down, Right, **▲**, **■**, **X**, **●**.

All Weapons

Pause the game, hold L2, and press Up, Left, Right, Down, **▲**, **■**, **●**, **X**.

Infinite Ammo

Pause the game, hold L2, and press Down, Left, Right, **X**, **■**, **●**.

Stealth Mode

Pause the game, hold L2, and press **X**, **X**, **■**, **■**, **▲**, **▲**, **●**, **●**, **X**, **X**.

FEAR EFFECT 2: RETRO HELIX

Cheat Mode

You must complete the game and start a new game. When you have control of Hana, you should open a console menu. Enter the following codes:

Effect	Code
Big Head	10397
All Weapons	11692
Infinite Ammo	61166

Art Galleries

At the title screen, enter the following codes for the respective disc to open the Art Gallery. You can find the Art Gallery in the Extras section of the Options menu.

Disc	Code
One	Left, Right, Up, Down, Down, ●
Two	Up, Up, R1, R1, R1, ■
Three	L1, R2, L1, R2, L1, ■
Four	●, ●, ■, L2, ■

HOT SHOTS GOLF

All Golfers and Courses

Turn on the system with no memory cards inserted. Before the Hot Shots Golf logo, hold L1 + L2 + R1 + R2 on controller 2. As the logo moves, press Up, Up, Down, Up, Left, Right, Right, Left, Up, Up, Down, Up, Left, Right, Right, Left.

HOT SHOTS GOLF 2

All Characters

Enter **2gsh** as your name.

THE ITALIAN JOB

Enter the following at the main menu, unless otherwise noted. Applause will indicate correct entry.

All Cheats

Press ▲, ●, ▲, ●, ▲, ■, ▲, ■

All Missions in Italian Job Mode

Press ●, ●, ▲, ■, ■.

All Missions in Challenge Mode

Press ■, ■, ▲, ●, ●, ■, ▲, ●.

All Missions in Checkpoint Mode

Press ●, ■, ▲, ■, ▲, ■, ▲, ■, ●.

All Missions in Destructor Mode

Press ▲, ■, ■, ▲, ■, ■, ▲, ● (3).

All Missions in Free Ride

Press ■, ▲, ■, ● (3), ▲, ●.

Level Select

In Career mode, pause the game, hold R1, and press ▲, Left, Left, ▲, ●, Up, Up, ■.

MAT HOFFMAN'S PRO BMX

During a session in a level, press Start. At the Pause menu, hold L1 and enter the following codes:

8 Minutes Added to Your Run Time

■, Up, ●, X

Entering the following codes will toggle the cheat on and off:

Big Tires

Down, ●, ●, Down

Slow

■, ▲, ●, X

Low Gravity

Up, Up, Up, Up

Special Bar Always Full

Left, Down, ▲, ●, Up, Left, ▲, ■

Grind Balance Bar

Left, ●, ■, ▲, ■, ●, X

Perfect Balance
■, Left, Up, Right

All scores Multiplied by 10
■, ●, ●, Up, Down, Down

All Scores Divided by 10
Down, Down, Up, ●, ●, ■

Alternate Colors
Down, Down, Down, Down

Granny
Up, ■, **X**, **X**, Down, ●

NEED FOR SPEED 3: HOT PURSUIT

Enter the following as your name:

All Cars and Tracks
Enter **SPOILT**.

More Camera Views
Enter **SEEALL**.

El Nino
Enter **ROCKET**.

Jaguar XJR-15
Enter **LJAGX**.

Mercedes Benz CLK-GTR
Enter **AMGMRC**.

AutoCross Track
Enter **XCNTRY**.

Caverns Track
Enter **XCAV8**.

Empire City Track
Enter **MCITYZ**.

Scorpio-7 Track
Enter **GLDFSH**.

Space Race Track

Enter MNBEAM.

The Room Track

Enter PLAYTM.

NFL BLITZ 2001

VS Cheats

You must enter the following codes at the Versus screen by pressing the Turbo, Jump, and Pass buttons. For example, to get Infinite Turbo, press Turbo (x5), Jump (x1), Pass (x4), and Up.

Effect	Code
Tournament Mode (2-player game)	1,1,1 Down
Infinite Turbo	5,1,4 Up
Fast Turbo Running	0,3,2 Left
Power-up Offense	3,1,2 Up
Power-up Defense	4,2,1 Up
Power-up Teammates	2,3,3 Up
Power-up Blockers	3,1,2 Left
Super Blitzing	0,4,5 Up
Super Field Goals	1,2,3 Left
Invisible	4,3,3 Up

No Random Fumbles	4,2,3 Down
No First Downs	2,1,0 Up
No Interceptions	3,4,4 Up
No Punting	1,5,1 Up
Allow Stepping Out of Bounds	2,1,1 Left
Fast Passes	2,5,0 Left
Late Hits	0,1,0 Up
Show Field Goal %	0,0,1 Down

Effect	Code
Show Punt Hangtime Meter	0,0,1 Right
Hide Receiver Name	1,0,2 Right
Big Football	0,5,0 Right
Big Head	2,0,0 Right
Huge Head	0,4,0 Up

Team Tiny Players	3,1,0 Right
Team Big Players	1,4,1 Right
Team Big Heads	2,0,3 Right

Effect	Code
Weather: Snow	5,2,5 Down
Weather: Rain	5,5,5 Right
No Highlighting on Target Receiver	3,2,1 Down
Red, White, and Blue Ball	3,2,3 Left
Unlimited Throw Distance	2,2,3 Right
Deranged Blitz Mode (1-player game)	2,1,2 Down
Ultra Hard Mode (1-player game)	3,2,3 Up
Smart CPU Opponent (1-player game)	3,1,4 Down
Always Quarterback	2,2,2 Left
Always Receiver	2,2,2 Right
Cancel Always Quarterback/Receiver	3,3,3 Up
Show More Field (2-player agreement)	0,2,1 Right
No CPU Assistance (2-player agreement)	0,1,2 Down
Power-up Speed (2-player agreement)	4,0,4 Left

Effect	Code
Hyper Blitz (2-player agreement)	5,5,5 Up
No Play Selection (2-player agreement)	1,1,5 Left
Super Passing (2-player agreement)	4,2,3 Right

Team Playbooks

Effect	Code
Arizona Cardinals	1,0,1 Left
Atlanta Falcons	1,0,2 Left
Baltimore Ravens	1,0,3 Left
Buffalo Bills	1,0,4 Left
Carolina Panthers	1,0,5 Left
Chicago Bears	1,1,0 Left
Cincinnati Bengals	1,1,2 Left
Cleveland Browns	1,1,3 Left
Dallas Cowboys	1,1,4 Left
Denver Broncos	1,1,5 Right
Detroit Lions	1,2,1 Left
Green Bay Packers	1,2,2 Left
Indianapolis Colts	1,2,3 Up
Jacksonville Jaguars	1,2,4 Left
Kansas City Chiefs	1,2,5 Left
Miami Dolphins	1,3,1 Left
Minnesota Vikings	1,3,2 Left
New England Patriots	1,3,3 Left
New Orleans Saints	1,3,4 Left
New York Giants	1,3,5 Left
New York Jets	1,4,1 Left
Oakland Raiders	1,4,2 Left
Philadelphia Eagles	1,4,3 Left
Pittsburgh Steelers	1,4,4 Left
San Diego Chargers	1,4,5 Left
San Francisco 49ers	1,5,1 Left
Seattle Seahawks	1,5,2 Left
St. Louis Rams	1,5,3 Left
Tampa Bay Buccaneers	1,5,4 Left
Tennessee Titans	1,5,5 Left
Washington Redskins	2,0,1 Left

NFL GAMEDAY 2002

Codes

Select Code Entry from the options and enter the following:

Code	Effect
5280 CLUB	Mile High Stadium

GRUDGE MATCH	GameDay stadium
989 SPORTS	989 team
RED_ZONE	Redzone team
ALL BOBO	Everyone named Bobo

BASKETBALL	Players named after NBA players
OVAL OFFICE	Players named after Presidents
EURO LEAGUE	Players named after NFL Europe players
EVEN STEVEN	Even teams
BIG PIG	Big football
TINY	Big players
MUNCHKINS	Small players
PENCILS	Thin and tall
ENDURANCE	More endurance
FATIGUE	Reduce fatigue
MR GLASS	Injured hamstring

Code	Effect
MR FURIOUS	Hop-a-long

Code	Effect
POP WARNER	Players float

Code	Effect
LINE BUSTER	Better defensive line
SUPER FOOT	Better Running Back
FASHION SHOW	Cheerleader pictures after the game

Code	Effect
CREDITS	Credits

NFL GAMEDAY 2003

Easter Eggs

Code	Effect
BIG PIG	Big Football
LITTLE	Small Players
MUNCHKINS	Small Players
BIGBOYS	Big Players
PANCAKE	Flat Players
ENDURANCE	Better Endurance
EVEN	Even Teams
REDZONE	Redzone Names
ALL BOBO	Players Named Bobo
CREDITS	Credits

SPIDER-MAN 2: ENTER ELECTRO

Unlock All Cheats

Select Cheats from the Special Menu and enter **AUNTMAY**.

Unlock Costumes

Select Cheats from the Special Menu and enter **WASHMCHN**.

Unlock Gallery

Select Cheats from the Special Menu and enter **DRKROOM**.

Unlock Training

Select Cheats from the Special Menu and enter **CEREBRA**.

Unlock Levels

Select Cheats from the Special Menu and enter **NONJYMNT**.

Big Feet

Select Cheats from the Special Menu and enter **STACEYD**.

Big Head

Select Cheats from the Special Menu and enter **ALIEN**.

Debug Mode

Select Cheats from the Special Menu and enter **DRILHERE**.

What If

Select Cheats from the Special Menu and enter **VVISIONS**.

VV High Scores

Select Cheats from the Special Menu and enter **VVHISCRS**.

SPYRO: YEAR OF THE DRAGON

Pause your game and enter the following codes to get the desired effect:

2D Spyro

Left, Right, Left, Right, L1, R1, L1, R1, ■, ●

Enter the code again to change Spyro back to full 3D.

Big Head

Up, R1, Up, R1, Up, R1, ●, ●, ●, ●

Enter the code again to change Spyro's head back to normal.

Black Spyro

Up, Left, Down, Right, Up, ■, R1, R2, L1, L2, Up, Right, Down, Left, Up, Down

Blue Spyro

Up, Left, Down, Right, Up, ■, R1, R2, L1, L2, Up, Right, Down, Left, Up, X

Green Spyro

Up, Left, Down, Right, Up, ■, R1, R2, L1, L2, Up, Right, Down, Left, Up, ▲

Pink Spyro

Up, Left, Down, Right, Up, ■, R1, R2, L1, L2, Up, Right, Down, Left, Up, ■

Red Spyro

Up, Left, Down, Right, Up, ■, R1, R2, L1, L2, Up, Right, Down, Left, Up, ●

Yellow Spyro

Up, Left, Down, Right, Up, ■, R1, R2, L1, L2, Up, Right, Down, Left, Up, Up

Original Color Spyro

To change Spyro back to his original color, enter Up, Left, Down, Right, Up, ■, R1, R2, L1, L2, Up, Right, Down, Left, Up, Left.

Credits

Left, Right, Left, Right, Left, Right, ■, ●, ■, ●, ■, ●

Crash Bash Demo

Enter this code at the Title Screen. Once there, press L1 + R2 + ■.

TEST DRIVE 6

Enter the following codes as a name:

Effect	Code
$6,000,000	AKJGQ
All Cars	DFGY
All Tracks	ERERTH
All Quick Race Tracks	CVCVBM
No Quick Race Tracks	OCVCVBM
Shorter Tracks	QTFHYF
All Challenges	OPIOP
No Challenges	OPOIOP
Disable Checkpoint	FFOEMIT
Enable Checkpoint	NOEMIT
Stop the Bomber Mode	RFGTR

TEST DRIVE LE MANS

Cheat Codes

Enter the following as your name:

Code	Effect
FIRSTON	Win the race
MAYOU	1999 Audi R8R
POHLIN	1999 BMW V12 LMR

PINOU	1999 Toyota GT-1
NAIMAR	Spacecraft race

Code	Effect
BUGGYX	Replace X with a number between 1 and 8 to race as one of eight buggies

HOTDOG	Race as Hotdog in a race against other foods
FROMAGE	Race as Cheese in a race against other foods
PIE	Race as PorkPie in a race against other foods

PIZZA	Race as Pizza in a race against other foods
MM1 or MM8	Race as Spacecraft in Motor Mash race
MM2	Race as Jet in Motor Mash race
MM3	Race as Mad in Motor Mash race
MM4	Race as Taxi in Motor Mash race
MM5	Race as Bus in Motor Mash race
MM6	Race as Ice in Motor Mash race
MM7	Race as Submarine in Motor Mash race

| JACKPOT | Hawaiian Tropic girl |

TOMB RAIDER CHRONICLES

Unlock Unlimited Health, Ammo, and Weapons

While in the game, press Select to access your inventory screen. Highlight the Timex and enter the following secret code:

Hold Up + R1 + L1 + L2 + R2, and press ▲.

Unlock Every Item For Your Level

While in the game, press Select to access your inventory screen. Highlight the Timex and enter the following secret code:

Hold Down + R1 + L1 + L2 + R2, and press ▲.

This also gives you the Special Features option at the main menu.

Start at Second Adventure

Highlight the New Game option at the main menu, and enter the following secret code:

Hold L1 + Up, then press **X** to start at the Russian Base.

Start at Third Adventure

Highlight the New Game option at the main menu, and enter the following secret code:

Hold L2 + Up, then press **X** to start at the Black Isle.

Start at Fourth Adventure

Highlight the New Game option at the main menu, and enter the following secret code:

Hold R1 + Up, then press **X** to start at the Tower Block.

TONY HAWK'S PRO SKATER 2

Neversoft Characters

At the Main Menu, hold L1 and press Up, ■, ■, ▲, Right, Up, ●, ▲. This causes the wheel to spin. Create a skater, and give him the name of anyone on the Neversoft team. For example, name your skater Mick West and he'll appear. The best one is Connor Jewett, the son of Neversoft's President. (Don't change the appearance of the kid-sized skaters. It could crash your game.)

You must enter the following codes after pausing the game. While the game is paused, press and hold L1, and enter the codes.

Jet Pack Mode

Up, Up, Up, Up, **X**, ■, Up, Up, Up, Up, **X**, ■, Up, Up, Up, Up

Hold ▲ to hover.

Press **X** to turn on the Jetpack.

Press forward to move forward.

Fatter Skater

X (x4), Left, **X** (x4), Left, **X** (x4), Left

Thinner Skater

X (x4), ■, **X** (x4), ■, **X** (x4), ■

Toggle Blood On/Off

Right, Up, ■, ▲

Special Meter Always Yellow

X, ▲, ●, ●, Up, Left, ▲, ■

Super Speed Mode

Down, ■, ▲, Right, Up, ●, Down, ■, ▲, Right, Up, ●

Unlock Everything

X, X, X, ■, ▲, Up, Down, Left, Up, ■, ▲, X, ▲, ●, X, ▲, ●

Big Head

■, ●, Up, Left, Left, ■, Right, Up, Left

All Gaps

Down, Up, Left, Left, ●, Left, Up, ▲, ▲, Up, Right, ■, ■, Up, X

This will give you Private Carrera.

All Secret Characters

■, ●, Right, ▲, ●, Right, ●, ▲, Right, ■, Right, Up, Up, Left, Up, ■

Moon Physics

X, ■, Left, Up, Down, Up, ■, ▲

Double Moon Physics

Left, Up, Left, Up, Down, Up, ■, ▲, Left, Up, Left, Up, Down, Up, ■, ▲

$5000
X, Down, Left, Right, Down, Left, Right

100,000 Points in Competition
■, ●, Right, ■, ●, Right, ■, ●, Right

This will end the competition.

Access All Levels
Up, ▲, Right, Up, ■, ▲, Right, Up, Left, ■, ■, Up, ●, ●, Up, Right

Stats at 5
Up, ■, ▲, Up, Down

Stats at 6
Down, ■, ▲, Up, Down

Stats at 7
Left, ■, ▲, Up, Down

Stats at 8
Right, ■, ▲, Up, Down

Stats at 9
●, ■, ▲, Up, Down

Stats at 13
X, ▲, ●, X, X, X, ■, ▲, Up, Down

Stats at All 10s
X, ▲, ●, ■, ▲, Up, Down

Skip To Restart
■, ▲, Right, Up, Down, Up, Left, ■, ▲, Right, Up, Down, Up, Left, ●, Up, Left, ▲

Clear Game with Current Skater
●, Left, Up, Right, ●, Left, Up, Right, X, ●, Left, Up, Right, ●, Left, Up, Right

Kid Mode
●, Up, Up, Left, Left, ●, Up, Down, ■

Mirror Level

Up, Down, Left, Right, ▲, X, ■, ●, Up, Down, Left, Right, ▲, X, ■, ●

Perfect Balance

Right, Up, Left, ■, Right, Up, ■, ▲

Slo-Nic Mode

●, Up, ▲, ■, X, ▲, ●

Wireframe

Down, ●, Right, Up, ■, ▲

Sim Mode

●, Right, Up, Left, ▲, ●, Right, Up, Down

Smooth Shading

Down, Down, Up, ■, ▲, Up, Right

Disco Lights

Down, Up, ■, ●, Up, Left, Up, X

TONY HAWK'S PRO SKATER 3

The menu shakes if the following are entered correctly:

Big Head

Pause the game, hold L1 and press Up, ●, Down.

Thin Skater

Pause the game, hold L1 and press X (x4), ■, X(4), ■, X (x4), ■.

Fat Skater

Pause the game, hold L1 and press X (x4), Left, X (x4), Left, X (x4), Left.

Perfect Balance

Pause the game, hold L1 and press Up, Down, Up, Up, ▲, X, ▲, ▲.

Stud Mode

Pause the game, hold L1 and press ■, ▲, Up, Down, Right, Up, ■, ▲.

Full Special

Pause the game, hold L1 and press ▲, Right, Up, ■, ▲, Right, Up, ■, ▲.

10,000 Points

Pause the game, hold L1 and press ■, ●, Right, ■, ●, Right, ■, ●, Right.

Turbo

Pause the game, hold L1 and press press Left, Up, ■, ▲.

Slow Motion

Pause the game, hold L1 and press Left, Left, Up, Left, Left, Up, **X**.

Reversed Level

Pause the game, hold L1 and press Down, Down, ▲, Left, Up, ■, ▲

TWISTED METAL 4

Enter the following codes as passwords. You will hear a sound when entered correctly.

Effect	Code
Play as Sweet Tooth	START, R1, Right, Right, Left
Play as Crusher	Down, R1, Right, R1, L1
Play as Moon Buggy	START, ▲, Right, L1, START
Play as RC Car	Up, Down, Left, START, Right
Play as Super Axel	Up, Right, Down, Up, L1
Play as Minion	▲, L1, L1, Left, Up
Play as Super Auger	Left, ●, ▲, Right, Down
Play as Super Thumper	●, ▲, START, ●, Left
Play as Super Slamm	Right, L1, START, ●, START
Powerful special weapons	Up, START, ●, R1, Left
Very little traction	Down, ▲, Down, L1, R1
CPU targets humans	Right, ▲, Right, ▲, L1
All power-ups are Homing Missiles	R1, Right, Left, R1, Up
All power-ups are Napalms	Right, Left, R1, Right, ●
All power-ups are Power Missiles	Down, Down, ●, L1, Left
All power-ups are Remote Bombs	Up, Right, Down, L1, ▲
CPU ignores health	L1, Left, Right, ●, Right
Extra fast weapons	R1, L1, Down, START, Down
Faster health regeneration	▲, L1, Down, ▲ Up
God Mode	Down, Left, L1, Left, Right
No health in deathmatch	▲, Down, ▲, ●, ▲

Effect	Code
No health in tournament and deathmatch	Down, R1, Down, START, ●
No power-ups	●, START, Left, L1, START

THE WEAKEST LINK

Final Round Passwords

To get the following players in the Final Round, highlight the indicated character in round 2 and press ● to open the password screen. Enter the password.

Player	Highlight	Password
Allen	Ruth	Right, Right, Left, Left, Up, Up, Left, Right
Amber	Barry	Right, Right, Up, Right, Left, Down, Right, Right
Angela	Steve	Left, Left, Down, Right, Up, Left, Down, Up
Cindy	Eddie	Right, Up, Up, Down, Up, Down, Down, Up
Eddie	Jules	Right, Up, Left, Down, Left, Up, Up, Down
Evelyn	Eddie	Right, Right, Down, Down, Right, Up, Right, Left
Jenny	Frank	Right, Right, Down, Up, Up, Left, Right, Down
Jojo	Ruth	Down, Right, Right, Left, Down, Right, Up, Down
Jules	Karen	Left, Down, Down, Right, Right, Right, Up, Down
Karen	Gary	Down, Down, Right, Up, Up, Down, Down, Up
Mary	Tim	Up, Right, Up, Left, Down, Right, Up, Down
Nick	Ruth	Down, Right, Up, Left, Up, Left, Left, Right
Ravi	Tony	Left, Left, Left, Up, Down, Left, Up, Down
Ruth	Barry	Up, Down, Up, Down, Left, Right, Down, Down
Samantha	Angela	Down, Down, Right, Right, Up, Right, Down, Up
Steve	Tim	Left, Left, Up, Right, Down, Right, Down, Up
William	Jules	Down, Right, Right, Left, Up, Left, Up, Down

WORLD'S SCARIEST POLICE CHASES

All Bonuses

At the main menu, press Left, Right, L1, R1, ●, ■, L2, L2.

Level Select

At the main menu, press Down, Up, Left, Right, X, ▲, ●, ■.

THE GAMES

Xbox™

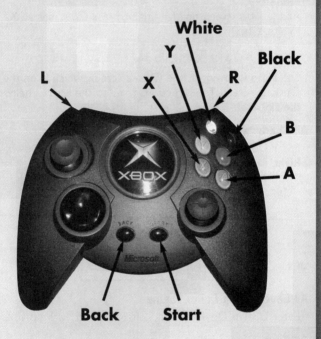

4X4 EVOLUTION 2

Level Select

At the Title screen or Main menu, press X, X, White, White, Y, Y, White, X, Y, Y, X, White.

Extra Money

At the Title screen or Main menu, press Y, X, White, Y, X, White, X, X, Y, White, X, Y.

Reputation

At the Title screen or Main menu, press Y, Y, White, X, X, White, Y (x3), X (x3).

AGGRESSIVE INLINE

Enter the following at the Cheats screen, which is on the Options screen. The directions refer to the arrows below the alphabet.

All Characters

Enter Down, Right, Right, Down, Left, Down, Left, Down, Right, Right, Right.

All Levels, Park Editor Themes

Enter Up, Up, Down, Down, Left, Right, Left, Right, BABA.

All Keys

Enter **SKELETON**.

Invulnerable

Enter **KHUFU**.

Perfect Grind Balance
  Enter **BIGUPYASELF**.

Perfect Handplant Balance
  Enter **JUSTINBAILEY**.

Perfect Manual Balance
  Enter **QUEZDONTSLEEP**.

Regenerating Juice
  Enter Left, Left, Right, Right, Left, Right, Down, Up, Up, Down, AI.

Juice Remains After Crash
  Enter **BAKABAKA**.

Better Wallrides
  Enter Up, Down, Up, Down, Left, Right, Left, Right, ABABS.

Faster Spin
  Enter Left, Left, Left, Left, Right, Right, Right, Right, Left, Right, Left, Right, Up.

BLADE 2

Level Select
  Hold L and press Down, Up, Left, Left, B, Right, Down, X at the Main menu.

Unlimited Health
  Pause game play, then hold L and press Y, X, Y, X, Y, B, Y, B.

Unlimited Rage
  Pause game play, then hold L and press Left, Down, Left, Down, Right, Up, Right, Up.

All Weapons
  Hold L and press X, B, Down, Left, B, B, Y at the Main menu.

Unlimited Ammunition

Pause the game, then hold L and press Left, B, Right, X, Up, Y, Down, A.

Daywalker Difficulty Setting

Hold L and press Left, B, Up, Down, X, B, A at the Main menu.

Escorted NPCs are Invincible

Pause the game, then hold L and press X, B, Y, A, X, B, Y, A. This code can only be activated in levels during which you're escorting NPCs.

BLOOD WAKE

All Boats

At the Title screen, press Up, Down, Left, Right, Left trigger, B, X, X, Right thumbstick, START.

All Levels

At the Title screen, press X, Y, Up, Right, Left, Down, Up, Down, Left trigger, Left trigger, START.

All Battle Modes

At the Title screen, press Y, A, X, B, Left thumbstick, Right thumbstick, Black, White, Right trigger, Right trigger, START.

Import Boat

At the Title screen, press Y, B, X, A, Left trigger, Right trigger, Left, Right, Left thumbstick, Right thumbstick, START.

Invulnerability

At the Title screen, press Left thumbstick, Right thumbstick, Down, Left, Down, Left, B, Y, START.

Unlimited Ammo

At the Title screen, press Black, White, Left trigger, Right trigger, Right thumbstick, Right thumbstick, Y, X, START.

Unlimited Turbo

At the Title screen, press Up, Up, Down, Down, Left, Right, Left, Right, B, A, START.

Puffer Fish

At the Title screen, press A, B, Black, White, Y, X, Right thumbstick, Right thumbstick, Left thumbstick, Left thumbstick.

Blood Ball Mode

At the Title screen press X, Y, White, Black, B, A, Left, Up, Right, Down.

Rubber Duck Mode

At the Title screen press Right thumbstick, Left thumbstick, Right Trigger, Left Trigger, Black, White, Up, Down, Left, Right.

BRUCE LEE: QUEST OF THE DRAGON

Bruce's Challenges

At the Title screen press X, Y, X, Y, X, X, Y, Y, Left thumbstick, Right thumbstick.

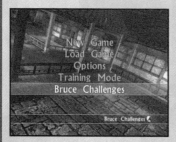 

BUFFY THE VAMPIRE SLAYER

Invincible

At the Extras menu, press Y, White, Black, Black, White, Y Black (x3), Y (x3). You hear a scream when the code is entered correctly.

Slayer Power

At the Extras menu, press Y (x3), Black (x3), Y, White, Black, Black, White, Y. You hear a scream when the code is entered correctly.

Arenas

At the Extras menu, press Y, Y, White, Black, Black, Y (x5), White, Black. You should hear a scream if entered correctly.

Dark Buffy in Arena Mode

At the Extras menu, press Black, White, Y, Y, Black, Black, White, Black, Black, White, Black, Black, White, Black (x3), White, White. You hear a scream when the code is entered correctly.

CRAZY TAXI 3 HIGH ROLLER

Expert Mode

At the Character Select screen, highlight a driver, hold White + Black and press A.

No Arrows

At the Character Select screen, highlight a driver, hold White and press A.

No Destination Mark

At the Character Select screen, highlight a driver, hold Black and press A.

Unlock Everything

Plug a controller into the fourth slot. At the Main menu press and hold L + R + Left thumbstick + Right thumbstick + X + Y until you hear "Congratulations."

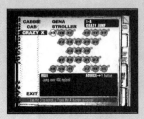

DEAD TO RIGHTS

Chapter Select

At the Main menu, press Up, Down, Up, Down, Left, Right, Right, Y, X, X. Select Chapters at the bottom of the menu to select a destination.

DRIVEN

All Drivers

At the Main menu, press Up, Down, Right, Right, Left, Up, Up, Down.

All Tracks

At the Main menu, press Up, Up, Left, Down, Left, Right, Right, Up.

All Chapters in Story Mode

At the Main menu, press Down, Left, Up, Right, Right, Up, Down, Left.

All Championships in Arcade Mode

At the Main menu, press Right, Left, Up, Right, Down, Down, Left, Left.

All Championships in Multiplayer Mode

At the Main menu, press Left, Down, Left, Up, Right, Left, Down, Right.

THE ELDER SCROLLS MORROWIND

During gameplay, press B to access the options. Then enter the following from the Statistics screen.

Raise Health Level

Highlight the health bar and press Black, White, Black, Black, Black, hold A.

Raise Magicka Level

Highlight the Magicka Bar and press Black, White, White, Black, White, hold A.

Raise Fatigue Level

Highlight the Fatigue Bar and press Black, Black, White, White, Black, hold A.

ENCLAVE

God Mode and Complete Mission

Pause the game and press X, Y, X, X, Y, Y, X, Y, X, X, Y, Y.

Dark Campaign

At the Episode Select screen press X, Y, Y, X, X, Y, X, Y.

FUZION FRENZY

First person mode

Pause the game, hold L and press Y, B, Y, B. Enter the code again to disable it.

Mutant Mode

Pause the game, hold L and press Y, B, X, X. Enter the code again for Mutant Mode 2, once again for Mutant Mode 3, and yet a fourth time to disable Mutant Mode.

Welsh

Pause the game, hold L and press Y, Y, Y, Y. Enter the code again to disable it.

Squeaky voices:

Pause the game, hold L and press Y, X, Y, Y. Enter the code again to disable it.

GUNMETAL

Mission Select

At the Mission Select screen, press Left Thumbstick, Black, R, Right Thumbstick, White, L.

Mission Skip

During a mission, press Left Thumbstick, White, White, Back, Right Thumbstick, White.

Alternate Music

At the Title screen, press Left Thumbstick, Left Thumbstick, Right Thumbstick, Right Thumbstick, L, R.

HUNTER THE RECKONING

All Weapons

During gamplay, press B, Up, Left, Down, Right, B, B.

Full Weapon Damage

During gameplay, press Down, Down, B, Y, Down, Down.

Sound From Game

During gameplay, press Left, Left, B or Right, Right, B.

KELLY SLATER'S PRO SURFER

Select Cheats from the Extras menu and enter the following cell phone numbers. Turn them on and off by selecting Toggle Cheat.

Max Stats

Enter 2125551776.

High Jump

Enter 2175550217.

Perfect Balance

Enter **2135555721**.

First-Person View

Enter **8775553825**. Select Camera Settings from the
Options menu.

Trippy

Enter **8185551447**.

Mega Cheat

Enter **7145558092**.

All Levels

Enter **3285554497**.

All Suits

Enter **7025552918**.

All Surfers

Enter **9495556799**.

All Tricks

Enter **6265556043**.

Surfers

Enter the following to access different surfers.

Surfer	Cell Number
Freak	3105556217

Tiki God	8885554506

Surfer	Cell Number
Tony Hawk	3235559787

Travis Pastrana	8005556292

LEGACY OF KAIN: BLOOD OMEN 2

Begin Game with Soul Reaver and Iron Armor

At the Main menu press White, Black, L, R, X, B, Y.

LEGENDS OF WRESTLING

All Wrestlers

At the Main menu, press Up, Up, Down, Down, Left, Right, Left, Right, Y, Y, X.

THE LORD OF THE RINGS: THE FELLOWSHIP OF THE RING

Unlimited Ring Charges for Frodo

During gameplay, press Y, B, A, B, Y, X.

Unlimited Ammo

During gameplay, press X, B, Y, A, X, B.

Unlimited Health

During gameplay, quickly press Y, A, X, B, A, Y.

MAT HOFFMAN'S PRO BMX 2

Level Select

At the Title screen press Y, Right, Right, B, Down, Y. This code works for Session, Free Ride, and Multiplayer modes.

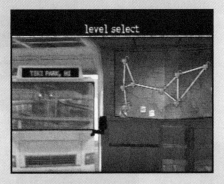

Boston, MA Level (Road Trip)

At the Title screen press Y, Up, Down, Down, Up, Y.

Chicago, IL Level (Road Trip)

At the Title screen press Y, Up, B, Up, B, Y.

Las Vegas, NV Level (Road Trip)

At the Title screen press Y, R, Left, L, Right, Y.

Los Angeles, CA Level (Road Trip)

At the Title screen press Y, Left, B (x2), Left, Y.

New Orleans, LA Level (Road Trip)

At the Title screen press Y, Down, Right, Up, Left, Y.

Portland, Oregon Level (Road Trip)

At the Title screen press Y, A, A, B, B, Y.

Day Smith

At the Title screen press B, Up, Down, Up, Down, Y.

Vanessa

At the Title screen press B, Down, Left, Left, Down, Y.

Big Foot

At the Title screen press B, Right, Up, Right, Up, Y.

The Mime

At the Title screen press B, Left, Right, Left, Right, Left.

Volcano

At the Title screen press B, Up, Up, A, Up, Up, A.

Elvis Costume

At the Title screen press X, L, L, Up, Up.

BMX Costume

At the Title screen press X, B, Left, Right, Left, X.

Tiki Battle Mode

At the Title screen press L, L, Down, R, A, L.

Mat Hoffman Videos

At the Title screen press R, Left, X, Left, X, Left, R.

Joe Kowalski Videos

At the Title screen press R, Up, A, B, Down, R.

Rick Thorne Videos

At the Title screen press R, L, Right, R, Left, R.

Mike Escamilla Videos

At the Title screen press R, X, A, A, X, A, A, R.

Simon Tabron Videos

At the Title screen press R, L, L, R, L, L, R.

Xbox™

Kevin Robinson Videos

At the Title screen press R, A, B, Down, Up, R.

Cory Nastazio Videos

At the Title screen press R, Y, X, X, Y (x3), R.

Ruben Alcantara Videos

At the Title screen press R, Left, Right, Left, Right, Left, Right, R.

Seth Kimbrough Videos

At the Title screen press R, Up, Up, X (x3), R.

Nate Wessel Videos

At the Title screen press R, Down, B, X, Down, B, X, R.

Big Ramp Video

At the Title screen press R, Up, Down, Left, A, A, A, R.

Day Flatland Video

At the Title screen press R, X, Left, Left, Y, Right, Right, R.

All Music

At the Title screen press L, Left, Left, Right (x3), A, A.

MAX PAYNE

Cheats

During gameplay, press Back to access the menu. Hold L + R and press the Left Analog Stick + the Right Analog Stick, White, Black, Black, White, White, Black.

MIKE TYSON HEAVYWEIGHT BOXING

Platinum Unlock

At the Title screen press X, B, L, R. This unlocks all Modes, all Boxers, and all Arenas.

Big Head Mode

At the Title screen press X, B, Up, Down.

Small Head Mode

At the Title screen press X, B, Down, Up.

2-D Mode

At the Title screen, press Down, Up, B, X.

Super Mutant Mode

At the Title screen, press X, Left, Up, Y.

Fun Custom Boxer Textures

At the Title screen, press L, R, A, A, Y, A.

Unlock Codies Credits

At the Title screen, press A, Y, X, B.

MLB SLUGFEST 20-03

At the Match-Up screen, use X, Y and B to enter the following codes, then press the appropriate direction. For example, for Rubber Ball press X (x2), Y (x4), B (x2), then press Up.

Code	Enter
Tournament Mode	1 1 1 Down
Big Head	2 0 0 Right
Tiny Head	2 0 0 Left
Unlimited Turbo	4 4 4 Down
No Fatigue	3 4 3 Up
Max Batting	3 0 0 Left
Max Power	0 3 0 Left
Max Speed	0 0 3 Left
Extra Time After Plays	1 2 3 Up
Log Bat	0 0 4 Up
Mace Bat	0 0 4 Left
Wiffle Bat	0 0 4 Right
Rubber Ball	2 4 2 Up
Softball	2 4 2 Down

Code	Enter
Roman Coliseum	3 3 3 Up

Pinto Team	2 1 0 Right

Eagle Team	2 1 2 Right

Rocket Park Stadium	3 2 1 Up

Todd McFarlane Team	2 2 2 Right

Code	Enter
Horse Team	2 1 1 Right

| Lion Team | 2 2 0 Right |

| Team Terry Fitzgerald | 3 3 3 Right |

NASCAR HEAT 2002

Hardcore Realism Mode

At the Main menu press Up, Down, Left, Right, White, Up, Down.

Wireframe Cars

At the Main menu press Up, Down, Left, Right, White, Right, Left.

Mini Cars

At the Main menu press Up, Down, Left, Right, White, Down, Up.

High Suspension

At the Main menu press Up, Down, Left, Right, White, Left, Right.

Credits

At the Main menu press Up, Down, Left, Right, White, Left, Left.

Paintballs (Single Race or Head-to-Head)

At the Race Day screen press Up, Down, Left, Right, White, Up, Up. Press Up to fire a paintball.

NASCAR THUNDER 2002

Extra Drivers

At the driver creation screen enter the following names:

Audrey Clark	Dave Nichols	Mandy Misiak
Benny Parsons	Diane Grubb	Michelle Emser
Buster Auton	Dick Paysor	Rick Edwards
Cheryl King	Jim Hannigan	Rick Humphrey
Chuck Spicer	Joey Joulwan	Sasha Soares
Crissy Hillsworth	Josh Neelon	Scott Brewer
Daryl Wolfe	Katrina Goode	Tom Renedo
Dave Alpern	Ken Patterson	Traci Hultzapple
	Kristi Jones	Troi Hayes

NASCAR THUNDER 2003

Fantasy Drivers

Select Create-A-Car from the Features menu and enter **Extra Drivers** as a name.

Dale Earnhardt

Select Create-A-Car from the Features menu and enter **Dale Earnhardt** as a name.

NFL BLITZ 20-03

Cheats

Use L, R, and A to enter the following cheats, then press the indicated direction to enable the cheat. For example, for Super Field Goals (1 2 3 Left) press L, R (x2), A (x3), then press Left.

Effect	Code
Tournament Mode	1 1 1 Down
More Time To Enter Codes	2 1 2 Right
Extra Time	0 0 1 Right
See More Field	0 2 1 Right
Auto Icon Passing	0 0 3 Up
No Auto Icon Passing	0 0 3 Down
Extra Play For Offense	3 3 3 Down
Smart CPU Teammates (Always QB)	3 1 4 Down
2 Humans/Team (Always Receiver)	2 2 2 Left
2 Humans/Team	2 2 2 Right
No First Downs	2 1 0 Up
No Highlight Target Player	3 2 1 Down
No Interceptions	3 5 5 Up
No Punting	1 4 1 Up
No Random Fumbles	5 2 3 Down
No Replays	5 5 4 Right
No CPU Assist	0 1 2 Down
Allow Stepping Out of Bounds	2 1 1 Left
Butter Fingaz	3 4 5 Up
Infinite Turbo	4 1 5 Up
Faster Running Speed	0 3 2 Left
Fast Passes	2 4 0 Left
Super Blitzing	0 5 4 Up
Super Field Goals	1 2 3 Left
Power-Up Offense	4 1 2 Up
Power-Up Defense	4 2 1 Up
Power-Up Linemen	5 2 1 Up
Big Head	2 0 0 Right
Big Head Teams	2 0 3 Right

Effect	Code
Huge Heads	1 4 5 Left
Big Feet	0 2 5 Left
Power Loader	0 2 5 Right
Chimp Mode	0 2 5 Up
Noftle Mode	3 2 5 Up
Showtime Mode	3 5 1 Right
Weather: Snow	5 5 5 Left
Weather: Rain	5 5 5 Right
Clear Weather	1 2 3 Right
Ground Fog	2 3 2 Down
Chrome Ball	0 3 0 Down
Classic Ball	0 3 0 Left
Arctic Station	0 3 4 Down
Central Park	0 3 3 Right
Training Grounds	0 3 5 Up
Team: Armageddon	5 4 3 Right
Team: Bilders	3 1 0 Up
Team: Brew Dawgs	4 3 2 Down
Team: Crunch Mode	4 0 3 Right
Team: Gsmers	5 0 1 Up
Team: Midway	2 5 3 Right
Team: Neo Tokyo	3 4 4 Down
Team: Rollos	2 5 4 Up

Hidden Players

Enter the following ID and PIN to play as that character:

ID	PIN
BEAR	1985
CLOWN	1974
COWBOY	1996
DEER	1997
DOLPHIN	1972
EAGLE	1981
HORSE	1999
PATRIOT	2002
LION	1963
PINTO	1966

ID	PIN
PIRATE	2001
RAM	2000
TIGER	1977
VIKING	1977

NFL FEVER 2003

Enter the following case-sensitive names to unlock these teams and stadiums.

1989 49ers
Enter **Empire**.

1985 Bears
Enter **Sausage**.

1998 Broncos
Enter **Milehigh**.

1964 Browns
Enter **Bigrun**.

1977 Cowboys
Enter **Thehat**.

1993 Cowboys
Enter **Lonestar**.

1972 Dolphins
Enter **Perfect**.

1967 Packers
Enter **Cheese**.

1996 Packers
Enter **Green**.

1983 Raiders
Enter **Outlaws**.

1978 Steelers
Enter **Curtain**.

Chromides
Enter **Regulate**.

Commandos
Enter **Camo**.

Cows
Enter **Milk**.

Creampuffs
Enter **Cakewalk**.

Crocs
Enter **Crykie**.

Da Rulahs
Enter **Tut**.

Eruption
Enter **Lava**.

Firemen
Enter **Blazer**.

Gladiators
Enter **BigBack**.

Hackers
Enter **Axemen**.

King Cobras
Enter **Venom**.

Mimes
Enter **Silence**.

Monks
Enter **Robes**.

Pansies
Enter **Viola**.

Polars
Enter **Igloo**.

Samurai
Enter **Slasher**.

Skeletons
Enter **Stone**.

Soldiers
Enter **Helmet**.

Sorcerers
Enter **Spellboy**.

Spies
Enter **Target**.

Thunder Sheep
Enter **Flock**.

Tumbleweeds
Enter **Dusty**.

War Elephants
Enter **Horns**.

Wild Cats
Enter **Kitty**.

Winged Gorillas
Enter **Flying**.

Commandos Stadium
Enter **Barracks**.

Pansies Stadium
Enter **Flowery**.

Pyramid Stadium
Enter **Sphinx**.

Samurai Stadium
Enter **Warrior**.

Tumbleweed Stadium
Enter **Dustbowl**

OUTLAW GOLF

All Characters and Equipment

Start a game with the name Golf_Gone_Wild.

Increase Ball Size

During gameplay, hold R and press Up, Up, Up, Down.

Decrease Ball Size

During gameplay, hold R and press Down, Down, Down, Up.

Perfect Shot

During gamplay, hold R and press White, Back, White, Black, Back.

New Outfits

At the Character Select screen, hold L and press Y, Y, White, Y, Black, Y.

No Wind

During gameplay, hold R and press Up, Left, Down, Right, Up, Left, Down, Right, X, X.

Beating Token

During gameplay, hold R and press Black, X, Black, Black, X. This only works with 0 tokens.

PRISONER OF WAR

Select Passwords from the Main Menu and enter the following.

All Chapters
  Enter **GER1ENG5**.

Default Chapters
  Enter **DEFAULTM**.

Informed Of All Events
  Enter **ALLTIMES**.

Informed of Core Current Events
  Enter **CORETIMES**.

All Secrets
  Enter **FARLEYMYDOG**.

First-Person Mode
  Enter **BOSTON**.

Top Down Mode
  Enter **FOXY**.

Unlimited Goodies
  Enter **DINO**.

Guard Size
  Enter **MUFFIN**.

Guard Perception
  Enter **QUINCY**.

Defiance
  Enter **Fatty**.

Game Creation Date and Time
  Enter **DT**.

Jun 12 2002
22:23:50

OK

RALLISPORT CHALLENGE

Classic Class
  Create a profile named **TheGoodStuff**.

Expert Class

Create a profile named **WheelToWheel**.

REDCARD SOCCER 2003

All Teams, All Stadiums, and Finals Mode

Enter **BIGTANK** as a name.

SOCCER SLAM

Big Heads

At the Title screen, press R, L, Up, Up, Y, Y.

Maximum Power

At the Title screen, press L, R, Left, Right, Y, Y.

Unlimited Turbo

At the Title screen, press L, R, Right, Up, X, X.

Unlimited Spotlight

At the Title screen, press L, R, Down, Right, Y, X.

Big Hits

At the Title screen, press L, R, Up, Up, X, Y.

8-Ball

At the Title screen, press R, Right, Up, Up, Y, Y.

Beach Ball

At the Title screen, press R, Right, Right, Down, Y, X.

Black Box Ball

At the Title screen, press R, Left, Left, Down, X, X.

Crate Ball

At the Title screen, press R, Left, Down, Right, Y, X.

Eyeball Ball

At the Title screen, press R, Right, Down, Up, X, X.

Globe Ball

At the Title screen, press R, Right, Right, Left, X, X.

Kid's Block Ball

At the Title screen, press R, Left, Right, Right, Y, Y.

Kids Play Ball

At the Title screen, press R, Right, Up, Down, X, Y.

Old School Ball

At the Title screen, press R, Right, Left, Left, Y, X.

Remy's Head Ball

At the Title screen, press R, Left, Right, Left, X, Y.

Rob's Head Ball

At the Title screen, press R, Left, Up, Left, Y, X..

Rusty Can Ball

At the Title screen, press R, Left, Up, Up, Y, Y.

All Alternate Teams

At the Title screen, press X, Y, Down(4).

Alternate El Fuego Team

At the Title screen, press X, X, Down, Down, Right, Left.

Alternate Spirit Team

At the Title screen, press Y, Y, Down, Down, Left, Right.

Alternate Subzero Team

At the Title screen, press Y, Y, Down, Right, Left, Up.

Alternate Toxic Team

At the Title screen, press Y, X, Down, Up, Up.

Alternate Tsunami Team

At the Title screen, press X, Y, Down, Up, Right, Left.

Alternate Volta Team

At the Title screen, press Y, X, Down, Up, Down, Up.

All Stadiums

At the Title screen, press R, R, Right, Right, Up(5), X, X.

Alpen Castle Stadium
At the Title screen, press Up, Up, Up, Down, X, X.

Jungle Canopy Stadium
At the Title screen, press L, R, Up, Down, Left, Right, X, Y.

Pacific Atoll Stadium
At the Title screen, press Up, Up, Left, Left, Y, Y.

Reactor Core Stadium
At the Title screen, press Up, Left, Left, Right, X, Y.

Riviera Ruins Stadium
At the Title screen, press Up, Down, Down, Right, Y, X.

Tribal Oasis Stadium
At the Title screen, press L, R, Up, Up, Down, Down, X, X.

All Player Items
At the Title screen, press Left, X, Left, X, Left.

Angus' Items
At the Title screen, press Left, X, Right, X, Up.

Arsenault's Items
At the Title screen, press Left, Y, Up, Y, Down.

Boomer's Items
At the Title screen, press Left, Y, Left, X, Up.

Dante's Items
At the Title screen, press Left, X, Right, Y, Left.

Djimon's Items
At the Title screen, press Left, Y, Down, Y, Up.

Duke's Items
At the Title screen, press Left, Y, Up, X, Right.

El Diablo's Items
At the Title screen, press Left, X, Right, X, Down.

Half-Pint's Items
At the Title screen, press Left, Y, Up, X, Up.

Kahuna's Items

At the Title screen, press Left, Y, Right, Y, Right.

Kaimani's Items

At the Title screen, press Left, X, Down, X, Down.

Kiril's Items

At the Title screen, press Left, Y, Up, X, Left.

Lola's Items

At the Title screen, press Left, X, Left, Y, Down.

Madeira's Items

At the Title screen, press Left, Y, Down, X, Up.

Nova's Items

At the Title screen, press Left, Y, Down, Y, Right.

Raine's Items

At the Title screen, press Left, X, Up, X, Up.

Rico's Items

At the Title screen, press Left, X, Right, X, Right.

Rumiko's Items

At the Title screen, press Left, Y, Left, Y, Up.

Zari's Items

At the Title screen, press Left, Y, Left, Y, Right.

Modern Film Mode

At the Title screen, press Y, X, Y, X, Y, X, Right, Left, Right, Left, Right, Left.

Classic Film Mode

At the Title screen, press X, Y, X, Y, X, Y, Left, Right, Left, Right, Left, Right.

SPIDER-MAN THE MOVIE

Unlock Everything
Enter **ARACHNID**.

Small Character
Enter **SPIDERBYTE**.

Big Head and Feet
Enter **GOESTOYOURHEAD**.

Big Head Enemies
Enter **JOELSPEANUTS**.

Goblin-Style Costume
Enter **FREAKOUT**.

Mary Jane
Enter **GIRLNEXTDOOR**.

Scientist
Enter **SERUM**.

Police Officer
  Enter **REALHERO**.

Captain Stacey
  Enter **CAPTAINSTACEY**.

The Shocker
  Enter **HERMANSCHULTZ**.

Thug 1
  Enter **KNUCKLES**.

Thug 2
  Enter **STICKYRICE**.

Thug 3
  Enter **THUGSRUS**.

Unlimited Webbing
  Enter **ORGANICWEBBING**.

All Combat Controls
  Enter **KOALA**.

Matrix-Style Attacks
  Enter **DODGETHIS**.

Super Coolant
  Enter **CHILLOUT**.

Level Select
  Enter **IMIARMAS**.

Level Skip

Enter **ROMITAS**. Pause the game and select Next Level to advance.

Pinhead Bowling Training Level

Enter **HEADEXPLODY**.

First-Person View

Enter **UNDERTHEMASK**.

SPLASHDOWN

Select Options, hold R and press Up, Up, Down, Down, Left, Right, Left, Right, X, B, X, B. Then enter the following case-sensitive codes.

All Characters

Enter **AllChar**.

All Courses

Enter **Passport**.

All Wetsuits

Enter **LaPinata**.

Ending Movies

Enter **Festival**.

Max Performance Meter

Enter **PMeterGo**. You will still stall if you miss a buoy.

Tough AI

Enter **AllOutAI**.

CPU Can't Knock You Off

Enter **TopBird**.

Normal AI on Hard Tracks

Enter **Hobble**.

UFO Ghost in Time Trial

Enter **IBelieve**.

F-18 Ghost in Time Trial

Enter **F18**.

SSX TRICKY

Mix Master Mike

At the Main menu, hold L + R and press A, A, Right, A, A, Down, A, A, Left, A, A, Up. Pick anyone and that person will be replaced by Mix Master Mike.

Mallora Outfit and Board for Elise

At the Main menu, hold L + R and press A, A, Right, B, B, Down, Y, Y, Left, X, X, Up.

STREET HOOPS

Select Cheats from Game Settings and enter the following.

Brick City Clothing

Press R, Black, R, L, Y, X, R, L.

Clown Uniform

Press X, L, X, Y.

Cowboy Uniform

Press Y, White, White, R.

Elvis Uniforms

Press Y, Black, White, Black, Black, White, L, Black.

Kung Fu Uniform

Press Y, Y, X, L.

Pimp Uniforms

Press R, X, Y, Black.

Santa Uniform

Press White, Black, White, Black.

Tuxedo Uniform

Press Black, Black, Y, X.

Normal Ball

Press R, X, X, L.

ABA Ball

Press Y, White, X, White.

Court Select Ball

Press Y, X, Y, L, Y, X, X.

Black Ball

Press White, White, Y, Black.

Theft Mode (Easier Steals)

Press R, X (x3), R, Black, Y, White.

Block Party (Easier Blocks)

Press R, Y, Black, White.

Power Game

Press White, Y, Black, Y.

Fast Clock

Press Y, Y, Y, X, X, X, L, Black.

Perfect Field Goals

Press Y, Y, Y, X, X, X, R, White.

TEST DRIVE

SoundMAX and SPX Cars

Enter the San Francisco Drag Race. Select the Dodge Concept Viper and set a time record, then enter **SOUNDMAX** as your name.

G4 TV Viper

Enter the San Francisco Drag Race, set a time record and enter **KQXYKGVY** as your name.

TONY HAWK'S PRO SKATER 3

Select Cheats from the Options menu and enter the following case-sensitive codes.

All Movies

Enter **rollit**.

Complete Game with Selected Character

Enter **stiffcomp**.

All Characters

Enter **teamfreak**.

Max Stats

Enter **juice4me**.

All Decks

Enter **neverboard**.

Unlock Created Skaters

Enter **weeatdirt**. Create a new skater with the following names.

062287
80's Mark
Aaron Skillman
Alan Flores
Andrew Rausch
Andy Nelson
Braineaters
Brian Jennings
Captain Jennings
Chad Findley
Chris Glenn
Chris Rausch
Chris Ward
Connor Jewett

Crashcart

Darren Thorne
Dave Cowling
Dave Stohl
DDT
Eastside
Edwin Fong
Frogham
Gary Jesdanun
GMIAB
Gorilla
Grass Patch
Henry Ji
James Rausch
Jason Uyeda
Jeremy Anderson
Joel Jewett

Johnny Ow
Junki Saita
Kevin Mulhall
Lisa Davies
Mark Scott
Matthew Day
Mick West

Mike Ward

Mini Joel

Nicole Willick

Noel Hines

Nolan Nelson

Paul Robinson

Pete Day

Pimpin Frank

Rachael Day

Ralph D'Amato

Rastapopolous

Riley Hawk

Ryan McMahon

Sandy Jewett

Scott Pease

Skillzilla

Spencer Hawk

Stacey D

Steve Ganem
Steven Rausch
Trey Smith
William Pease

TOTALED!

Unlock All

Start up the game and as it loads press Up, Down, Left, Right, A.

Kill AI

As the game loads, press Left, Left, A.

Bot Gang Up

As the game loads, press Down, Up, A.

Infinite Nitros

As the game loads, press Right, Left, A.

No Nitros

As the game loads, press Right, Left, Left, A.

Jump

As the game loads, press Left, Right, A. Use Y to hop.

TUROK: EVOLUTION

Select Enter Cheats from the Cheats menu and enter the following.

All Cheats

Enter **FMNFB**.

Invincible

Enter **EMERPUS**.

All Weapons

Enter **TEXAS**. This code unlocks all of the available weapons for that particular level.

Unlimited Ammo

Enter **MADMAN**.

Level Select

Enter **SELLOUT**.

Invisibility

Enter **SLLEWGH**.

Big Heads

Enter **HEID**.

Zoo Mode

Enter **ZOO**.

Demo Mode/Mini-game

Enter **HUNTER**.

The Games

Nintendo GameCube™

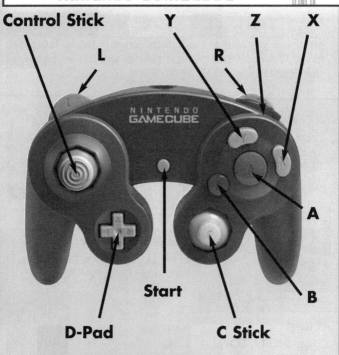

Control Stick

L

Y

R

Z

X

A

B

Start

D-Pad

C Stick

4X4 EVOLUTION 2

Level Select

At the Title screen, press X, X, Z, Z, Y, Y, Z, X, Y, Y, X, Z.

Money

At the Title screen, press Y, X, Z, Y, X, Z, X, X, Y, Z, X, Y.

Reputation

At the Title screen, press Y, Y, Z, X, X, Z, Y (x3), X (x3).

AGGRESSIVE INLINE

Enter the following at the Cheats screen, which is located in the Options. The directions refer to the arrows below the alphabet.

All Characters

Enter Down, Right, Right, Down, Left, Down, Left, Down, Right, Right, Right.

All Levels, Park Editor Themes

Enter Up, Up, Down, Down, Left, Right, Left, Right, BABA.

All Keys

Enter **SKELETON**.

Invulnerability

Enter **KHUFU**.

Perfect Grind Balance

Enter **BIGUPYASELF**.

Perfect Handplant Balance

Enter **JUSTINBAILEY**.

Perfect Manual Balance

Enter **QUEZDONTSLEEP**.

Regenerating Juice

Enter Left, Left, Right, Right, Left, Right, Down, Up, Up, Down, AI.

Juice Remains After Crash

Enter **BAKABAKA**.

Better Wallrides

Enter Up, Down, Up, Down, Left, Right, Left, Right, ABABS.

Faster Spin

Enter Left, Left, Left, Left, Right, Right, Right, Right, Left, Right, Left, Right, Up.

BATMAN VENGEANCE

Unlimited Electric Batarangs and Batarangs

Press L, R, Y, X at the Main menu.

BEACH SPIKERS

Select World Tour Mode and create a new team. Enter the following as the first player's name to unlock the outfits.

Daytona USA

Enter **DAYTONA**.

Fighting Vipers

Enter **FVIPERS**.

Phantasy Star Online 2

Enter **PHANTA2**.

Sega

Enter **OHTORII**.

Space Channel 5

Enter **ARAKATA**.

Virtua Cop

Enter **JUSTICE**.

CEL DAMAGE

Select Load from the Character Select screen and enter the following as a name.

Cheat Mode
Enter **PITA** or **FATHEAD**.

Invincibility
Enter **CODY**.

Pen and Ink Graphics
Enter **PENCILS**.

Plastic Graphics
Enter **FANPLASTIC**. Turn it on by selecting Rendering Modes from the Options screen.

Ranged Weapons
Enter **GUNSMOKE!**.

Melee Weapons
Enter **MELEEDEATH**.

Hazard Weapons
Enter **HAZARDOUS**.

Personal Weapons
Enter **UNIQUEWPNS**.

Move Power-ups
Enter **MOVEITNOW**.

All FMV
Enter **MULTIPLEX!**.

Brian the Brain and Space World
Enter **BRAINSALAD**.

Count Earl and Transylvania World
Enter **EARLSPLACE**.

T. Wrecks and Jungle World
Enter **TWRECKSPAD**.

Whack Angus and Desert World
Enter **WHACKLAND**.

DRIVEN

All Drivers

At the Main menu press Up, Down, Right, Right, Left, Up, Up, Down.

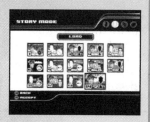

All Tracks

At the Main menu press Up, Up, Left, Down, Left, Right, Right, Up.

All Chapters in Story Mode

At the Main menu press Down, Left, Up, Right, Right, Up, Down, Left.

All Championships in Arcade Mode

At the Main menu press Right, Left, Up, Right, Down, Down, Left, Left.

All Championships in Multiplayer Mode

At the Main menu press Left, Down, Left, Up, Right, Left, Down, Right.

FREEKSTYLE

Select Enter Codes from the Options screen and enter the following.

All Characters, Outfits, Bikes, and Levels
Enter **LOKSMITH**.

All Characters
Enter **POPULATE**.

All Costumes
Enter **YARDSALE**.

All Bikes
Enter **WHEELS**.

All Tracks
Enter **TRAKMEET**.

Clifford Adoptante
Enter **COOLDUDE**.

Mike Jones
Enter **TOUGHGUY**.

Jessica Patterson
Enter **BLONDIE**.

Greg Albertyn
Enter **GIMEGREG**.

Unlimited Freekout
Enter **ALLFREEK**.

Quicker Freekout Meter
Enter **FIRESALE**.

Land a Trick for a Full Boost
Enter **MO BOOST**.

Infinite Boost
Enter **FREEBIE**.

No Bike
  Enter **FLYSOLO**.

Rider Wears a Helmet
  Enter **HELMET**.

Low Gravity
  Enter **FTAIL**.

Slow Motion
  Enter **WTCHKPRS**.

Burn It Up Track
  Enter **CARVEROK**.

Gnome Sweet Gnome Track
  Enter **CLIPPERS**.

Let It Ride Track
  Enter **BLACKJAK**.

Rocket Garden Track
  Enter **TODAMOON**.

Crash Pad FreeStyle Track
  Enter **WIDEOPEN**.

Burbs FreeStyle Track
  Enter **TUCKELLE**.

Bikes

Enter the following codes to access to different bikes.

Character	Bike	Code
Mike Metzger	Bloodshot	EYEDROPS
	Rock Of Ages	BRRRRRAP
	Rhino Rage	SEVENTWO
Brian Deegan	Mulisha Man	WHATEVER
	Heavy Metal	HEDBANGR
	Dominator	WHOZASKN
Leeann Tweeden	Hot Stuff	OVENMITT
	Trendsetter	STYLIN
	Seducer	GOODLOOK
Stefy Bau	Amore	HEREIAM
	Disco Tech	SPARKLES
	211	TWONEONE

Character	Bike	Code
Clifford Adoptante	Gone Tiki	SUPDUDE
	Island Spirit	GOFLOBRO
	Hang Loose	STOKED
Mike Jones	Beater	KICKBUTT
	Lil' Demon	HORNS
	Flushed	PLUNGER
Jessica Patterson	Speedy	HEKACOOL
	Charged Up	LIGHTNIN
	Racer Girl	TONBOY
Greg Albertyn	The King	ALLSHOOK
	National Pride	PATRIOT
	Champion	NUMBER

Outfits

Enter the following to access different outfits.

Character	Outfit	Code
Mike Metzger	Ecko MX	HELLOOOO
	All Tatted Up	BODYART
Brian Deegan	Muscle Bound	RIPPED
	Commander	SOLDIER
Leeann Tweeden	Fun Lovin'	THNKPINK
	Red Hot	SPICY
Stefy Bau	Playing Jax	KIDSGAME
	UFO Racer	INVASION
Clifford Adoptante	Tiki	WINGS
	Tankin' It	NOSLEEVE
Mike Jones	Blue Collar	BABYBLUE
	High Roller	BOXCARS
Jessica Patterson	Warming Up	LAYERS
	Hoodie Style	NOT2GRLY
Greg Albertyn	Sharp Dresser	ILOOKGUD
	Star Rider	COMET

GAUNTLET: DARK LEGACY

Cheat Codes

Enter the following codes as your name. You can only use one code at a time.

Effect	Code
10,000 Gold	10000K

9 Potions and Keys	ALLFUL
Pojo the Chicken	EGG911
Small Enemies	DELTA1
Invincibility	INVULN
Invisibility	000000
Anti-Death	1ANGEL
Full Turbo Meter	PURPLE
Faster	XSPEED
X-Ray	PEEKIN
Reflective Shots	REFLEX
3-Way Shot	MENAGE
Supershot	SSHOTS
Rapid Fire	QCKSHT

Secret Costumes

Enter the following codes as your name. Each code unlocks a different costume.

Class	Code
Dwarf	ICE600
	NUD069

Jester	KJH105
	PNK666
	STX222

Knight	ARV984
	BAT900
	CSS222
	DARTHC
	DIB626
	KAO292
	RIZ721
	SJB964
	STG333
	TAK118

Valkyrie	AYA555
	CEL721
	TWN300

Warrior	CAS400
	MTN200
	RAT333

Wizard	DES700
	GARM00
	GARM99
	SKY100
	SUM224

JEREMY MCGRATH SUPERCROSS WORLD

Need For Speed (Infinite Turbo)

At the Main menu press Down (x3), L, R, Z.

Feel Lighter (Less Gravity)

At the Main menu press Left, Right, Up, Down, B (x3).

Bouncy, Bouncy

At the Main menu press Up (x3), Y, Y, X, X.

Head Expands (Big Head)

At the Main menu press B, X, R, L, Right.

Drink Me (Smaller Riders)

At the Main menu press L, Z, Left, Right, B, B.

Tag, You're It

At the Main menu press Z, X, Z, X.

KELLY SLATER'S PRO SURFER

Select Cheats from the Extras screen and enter the following cell phone numbers. Turn them on and off by selecting Toggle Cheat.

Max Stats

Enter **2125551776**.

High Jump
Enter **2175550217**.

Perfect Balance
Enter **2135555721**.

First-Person View
Enter **8775553825**. Select Camera Settings from the Options screen.

Trippy
Enter **8185551447**.

Mega Cheat
Enter **7145558092**.

All Levels
Enter **3285554497**.

All Suits
Enter **7025552918**.

All Surfers
Enter **9495556799**.

All Tricks

Enter **6265556043**.

Surfers

Enter the following to unlock additional surfers.

Surfer	Cell Number
Freak	3105556217

Tiki God	8885554506

Tony Hawk	3235559787

Travis Pastrana	8005556292

LEGENDS OF WRESTLING

All Wrestlers

At the Main menu press Up, Up, Down, Down, Left, Right, Left, Right, Y, Y, X.

MLB SLUGFEST 2003

Cheats

At the Match-Up screen, use B, Y and X to enter the following codes, then press in the indicated direction. For example, for Rubber Ball press B (x2), Y (x4), X (x2), then press Up.

Effect	Code
Tournament Mode	111 Down
Big Head	200 Right
Small Heads	200 Left
Unlimited Turbo	444 Down
No Fatigue	343 Up
Max Batting	300 Left
Max Power	030 Left
Max Speed	003 Left
Extra Time After Plays	123 Up
No Contact Mode	433 Left
Log Bat	004 Up
Mace Bat	004 Left
Wiffle Bat	004 Right
Softball	242 Down
Rubber Ball	242 Up
Roman Coliseum	333 Up

Effect	Code
Monument Stadium	333 Down
Pinto Team	210 Right

Eagle Team	212 Right

Todd McFarlane Team	222 Right
Tiny Head	200 Left
Rocket Park Stadium	321 Up

Horse Team	211 Right

Effect	Code
Lion Team	220 Right

| Team Terry Fitzgerald | 333 Right |

MX SUPER FLY

Unlock Everything

At the Main menu press X, Y, L + X, X, L, Z, R + Y.

NASCAR THUNDER 2003

Fantasy Drivers

Select Create-A-Car from the Features menu and enter **Extra Drivers** as a name.

Dale Earnhardt

Select Create-A-Car from the Features menu and enter **Dale Earnhardt** as a name.

NBA STREET

Cheats

You can enter codes after selecting your players. Use the A, B, Y and X buttons to enter the codes. The first number corresponds to the number of times you press A, the second is for B, the third for Y, and the last for X. After entering the code, press any direction on the controller to enter the code. These numbers match up to icons on-screen as follows

0	Basketball
1	Record Player
2	Shoe
3	Backboard
4	Bullhorn

Nintendo GameCube™   N

For example, to enter the Big Heads code (4 1 2 1) you would press A (x4), B (x1), Y (x2), and X (x1). Then press any direction on the controller to activate the code.

Effect	Code
No Cheats	0 2 0 2
ABA Ball	0 0 1 2
WNBA Ball	0 0 2 3
NuFX Ball	0 0 3 4
EA Big Ball	0 0 4 1
Beach Ball	0 0 1 1
Medicine Ball	0 0 2 2
Volleyball	0 0 3 3
Soccer Ball	0 0 4 4
Big Heads	2 2 2 3
Tiny Heads	2 2 2 4
Tiny Players	2 2 2 1
Casual Uniforms	0 2 4 4
Authentic Uniforms	0 2 1 1
ABA Socks	2 2 2 2
Athletic Joe "The Show"	1 1 1 2
Springtime Joe "The Show"	1 1 1 0
Summertime Joe "The Show"	1 1 4 1
Player Names	1 1 0 1
No HUD Display	1 1 2 1
No Player Indicators	1 1 3 1
No Shot Indicator	1 1 1 3
No Shot Clock	2 2 2 0
Unlimited Turbo	1 2 2 0
No Juice	1 3 3 0
Easy Distance Shots	0 3 3 0
Harder Distance Shots	0 1 1 0
Captain Quicks	2 1 3 0
Mad Handles	2 3 1 0
Mega Dunking	0 4 4 0
Sticky Fingers	3 2 1 0
Super Swats	3 1 2 0
Ultimate Power	1 2 3 0
Less Blocks	0 1 2 0

Effect	Code
Less Steals	0 2 3 0
No 2-Pointers	0 1 3 0
No Alley-Oops	0 3 1 0
No Dunks	1 3 2 0
Less Gamebreakers	2 1 1 0
More Gamebreakers	2 3 3 0
No Gamebreakers	2 4 4 0
No Auto Replays	1 1 1 1
Explosive Rims	1 1 1 4

NFL BLITZ 20-03

Cheats

Use L, R, and A to enter the following cheats, then press the indicated direction to enable the cheat. For example, for Super Field Goals (1 2 3 Left) press L, R (x2), A (x3), and press Left.

Effect	Code
Tournament Mode	1 1 1 Down
More Time to Enter Codes	2 1 2 Right
Extra Time	0 0 1 Right
See More Field	0 2 1 Right
Auto Icon Passing	0 0 3 Up
No Auto Icon Passing	0 0 3 Down
Extra Play for Offense	3 3 3 Down
Smart CPU Teammates	3 1 4 Down
Always QB (2 Humans/Team)	2 2 2 Left
Always Receiver (2 Humans/Team)	2 2 2 Right
No First Downs	2 1 0 Up
No Highlight Target Player	3 2 1 Down

Effect	Code
No Interceptions	3 5 5 Up
No Punting	1 4 1 Up
No Random Fumbles	5 2 3 Down
No Replays	5 5 4 Right
No CPU Assist	0 1 2 Down
Allow Stepping Out of Bounds	2 1 1 Left
Butter Fingaz	3 4 5 Up
Infinite Turbo	4 1 5 Up
Faster Running Speed	0 3 2 Left
Fast Passes	2 4 0 Left
Super Blitzing	0 5 4 Up
Super Field Goals	1 2 3 Left
Power-Up Offense	4 1 2 Up
Power-Up Defense	4 2 1 Up
Power-Up Linemen	5 2 1 Up
Big Head	2 0 0 Right
Big Head Teams	2 0 3 Right
Huge Heads	1 4 5 Left
Big feet	0 2 5 Left
Power Loader	0 2 5 Right
Chimp Mode	0 2 5 Up

Effect	Code
Noftle Mode	3 2 5 Up
Showtime Mode	3 5 1 Right
Weather: Snow	5 5 5 Left
Weather: Rain	5 5 5 Right
Clear Weather	1 2 3 Right
Ground Fog	2 3 2 Down
Chrome Ball	0 3 0 Down
Classic Ball	0 3 0 Left

Effect	Code
Arctic Station	0 3 4 Down

Effect	Code
Central Park	0 3 3 Right
Training Grounds	0 3 5 Up
Team: Armageddon	5 4 3 Right

Effect	Code
Team: Bilders	3 1 0 Up
Team: Brew Dawgs	4 3 2 Down
Team: Crunch Mode	4 0 3 Right
Team: Gamers	5 0 1 Up
Team: Midway	2 5 3 Right
Team: Neo Tokyo	3 4 4 Down

Effect	Code
Team: Rollos	2 5 4 Up

Hidden Players

Enter the following ID and PIN to play as a particular character.

ID	PIN
BEAR	1985
CLOWN	1974

COWBOY	1996
DEER	1997

DOLPHIN	1972
EAGLE	1981

HORSE	1999
PATRIOT	2002

ID	PIN
LION	1963
PINTO	1966

PIRATE	2001
RAM	2000

TIGER	1977
VIKING	1977

REDCARD SOCCER 2003

All Teams, All Stadiums, and Finals Mode
Enter **BIGTANK** as a profile name.

ROCKET POWER: BEACH BANDITS

All Levels

Select Cheats from the Options screen and answer the multiple choice questions as Squid, Conroy, Tito Mikani, Maurice, Ocean Shores, Otto, Eddie: Prince of the Netherworld.

SCOOBY-DOO:
NIGHT OF 100 FRIGHTS

All Power-ups

Pause the game, hold L + R and press X, B, X, B, X, B (x3), X, X, B, X (x3).

Movie Gallery

Pause the game, hold L + R and press B (x3), X (x3), B, X, B.

Alternate Credits

Pause the game, hold L + R and press B, X, X, B, X, B.

Holidays

Change the system date to one of the following to change the appearance slightly.

January 1
July 4
October 31
December 25

SMUGGLER'S RUN: WAR ZONES

You hear a sound when the following codes are correctly entered. To disable the code, simply reenter it.

Low Gravity

Pause the game and press Z, R, Z, R, Right (x3).

Infinite Countermeasures

Pause the game and press Y, Y, Y, X, X, Z, Z.

Transparent Car

Pause the game and press Left, Right, Left, Right, Z, Z, R.

SOCCER SLAM

Big Heads

At the Title screen press R, L, Up, Up, Y, Y.

Maximum Power

At the Title screen press L, R, Left, Right, Y, Y.

Unlimited Turbo

At the Title screen press L, R, Right, Up, X, X.

Unlimited Spotlight

At the Title screen press L, R, Down, Right, Y, X.

Big Hits

At the Title screen press L, R, Up, Up, X, Y.

8-Ball

At the Title screen press R, Right, Up, Up, Y, Y.

Beach Ball

At the Title screen press R, Right, Right, Down, Y, X.

Black Box Ball

At the Title screen press R, Left, Left, Down, X, X.

Crate Ball

At the Title screen press R, Left, Down, Right, Y, X.

Eyeball Ball

At the Title screen press R, Right, Down, Up, X, X.

Globe Ball

At the Title screen press R, Right, Right, Left, X, X.

Kid's Block Ball

At the Title screen press R, Left, Right, Right, Y, Y.

Kids Play Ball

At the Title screen press R, Right, Up, Down, X, Y.

Old School Ball

At the Title screen press R, Right, Left, Left, Y, X.

Remy's Head Ball

At the Title screen press R, Left, Right, Left, X, Y.

Rob's Head Ball

At the Title screen press R, Left, Up, Left, Y, X.

Rusty Can Ball

At the Title screen press R, Left, Up, Up, Y, Y.

All Alternate Teams

At the Title screen press X, Y, Down (x4).

Alternate El Fuego Team

At the Title screen press X, X, Down, Down, Right, Left.

Alternate Spirit Team

At the Title screen press Y, Y, Down, Down, Left, Right.

Alternate Subzero Team

At the Title screen press Y, Y, Down, Right, Left, Up.

Alternate Toxic Team

At the Title screen press Y, X, Down, Up, Up.

Alternate Tsunami Team

At the Title screen press X, Y, Down, Up, Right, Left.

Alternate Volta Team

At the Title screen press Y, X, Down, Up, Down, Up.

All Stadiums

At the Title screen press R, R, Right, Right, Up (x5), X, X.

Alpen Castle Stadium

At the Title screen press Up, Up, Up, Down, X, X.

Jungle Canopy Stadium

At the Title screen press L, R, Up, Down, Left, Right, X, Y.

Pacific Atoll Stadium

At the Title screen press Up, Up, Left, Left, Y, Y.

Reactor Core Stadium

At the Title screen press Up, Left, Left, Right, X, Y.

Riviera Ruins Stadium

At the Title screen press Up, Down, Down, Right, Y, X.

Tribal Oasis Stadium

At the Title screen press L, R, Up, Up, Down, Down, X, X.

All Player Items

At the Title screen press Left, X, Left, X, Left.

Angus' Items

At the Title screen press Left, X, Right, X, Up.

Arsenault's Items

At the Title screen press Left, Y, Up, Y, Down.

Boomer's Items

At the Title screen press Left, Y, Left, X, Up.

Dante's Items

At the Title screen press Left, X, Right, Y, Left.

Djimon's Items

At the Title screen press Left, Y, Down, Y, Up.

Duke's Items

At the Title screen press Left, Y, Up, X, Right.

El Diablo's Items

At the Title screen press Left, X, Right, X, Down.

Half-Pint's Items

At the Title screen press Left, Y, Up, X, Up.

Kahuna's Items

At the Title screen press Left, Y, Right, Y, Right.

Kaimani's Items

At the Title screen press Left, X, Down, X, Down.

Kiril's Items

At the Title screen press Left, Y, Up, X, Left.

Lola's Items

At the Title screen press Left, X, Left, Y, Down.

Madeira's Items

At the Title screen press Left, Y, Down, X, Up.

Nova's Items

At the Title screen press Left, Y, Down, Y, Right.

Raine's Items

At the Title screen press Left, X, Up, X, Up.

Rico's Items

At the Title screen press Left, X, Right, X, Right.

Rumiko's Items

At the Title screen press Left, Y, Left, Y, Up.

Zari's Items

At the Title screen press Left, Y, Left, Y, Right.

Modern Film Mode

At the Title screen press Y, X, Y, X, Y, X, Right, Left, Right, Left, Right, Left.

Classic Film Mode

At the Title screen press X, Y, X, Y, X, Y, Left, Right, Left, Right, Left, Right.

SPIDER-MAN THE MOVIE

Unlock Everything
  Enter **ARACHNID**.

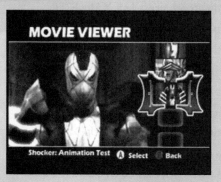

Small Character
  Enter **SPIDERBYTE**.

Big Head and Feet
  Enter **GOESTOYOURHEAD**.

Big Head Enemies
  Enter **JOELSPEANUTS**.

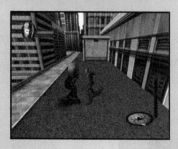

Goblin-Style Costume
  Enter **FREAKOUT**.

Mary Jane
  Enter **GIRLNEXTDOOR**.

Scientist
  Enter **SERUM**.

Police Officer

Enter **REALHERO**.

Captain Stacey

Enter **CAPTAINSTACEY**.

The Shocker

Enter **HERMANSCHULTZ**.

Thug #1

Enter **KNUCKLES**.

Thug #2

Enter **STICKYRICE**.

Thug #3

Enter **THUGSRUS**.

Unlimited Webbing

Enter **ORGANICWEBBING**.

All Combat Controls

Enter **KOALA**.

Matrix-Style Attacks
Enter **DODGETHIS**.

Super Coolant
Enter **CHILLOUT**.

Level Select
Enter **IMIARMAS**.

Level Skip
Enter **ROMITAS**. Pause the game and select Next Level
to advance.

Pinhead Bowling Training Level
Enter **HEADEXPLODY**.

First-Person View
Enter **UNDERTHEMASK**.

SPY HUNTER

Saliva: The Spy Hunter Theme Movie

Enter the Agent name as **GUNN**. After the name disappears, enter your name and select System Options at the next screen to access the movie.

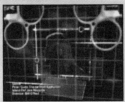

Early Test Animatic Movie

Enter the Agent name as **WOODY**. After the name disappears, enter your name and select System Options at the next screen to access the movie.

SSX TRICKY

Unlock Everything

At the Main menu, hold L + R and press A, B, Z, X, Y, Z, B, Y, Z, X, A, Z. Then release L + R.

Full Stats

At the Main menu, hold L + R and press B, B, Z, B, B, Z, A, A, Z, A, A, Z. Then release L + R.

Mix Master Mike

At the Main menu, hold L + R and press A, A, Z, A, A, Z, A, A, Z, A, A, Z. Then release L + R. Choose anyone, and he/she will be replaced by Mix Master Mike.

Elise's Mallora Board and Outfit

At the Main menu, hold L + R and press A, A, Z, X, X, Z, B, B, Z, Y, Y, Z. Then release L + R.

TONY HAWK'S PRO SKATER 3

All Cheats

Select Cheats from the Options menu and enter
MARKEDCARDS.

Max Stats

Select Cheats from the Options menu and enter
MAXMEOUT.

All Movies

Select Cheats from the Options menu and enter **POP-CORN**.

TOP GUN COMBAT ZONES

All Levels and Planes

Enter **SHPONGLE** as your callsign.

TUROK: EVOLUTION

Select Enter Cheats from the Cheats menu and enter the following.

All Cheats
Enter **FMNFB**.

Invincibility
Enter **EMERPUS**.

All Weapons
Enter **TEXAS**. This unlocks all of the available weapons for that particular level.

Unlimited Ammo
Enter **MADMAN**.

Level Select
Enter **SELLOUT**.

Invisibility
Enter **SLLEWGH**.

Big Heads
Enter **HEID**.

Zoo Mode
 Enter **ZOO**.

Demo Mode/Mini-game
 Enter **HUNTER**.

XGIII EXTREME G RACING

All Tracks
 At the Main menu press L, L, R, R, Z, Z, L + R + Z.

Infinite Ammunition
 At the Main menu press L, R, L, R, L + R, Z.

Double Prize Money
 At the Main menu press L, R, Z, L, R, Z, L + R.

Infinite Shield
 At the Main menu press L + R, Z, L + R, Z.

Will Win This Race
 At the Main menu press L + R + Z, L + R, Z, L + R + Z.

The Games

Game Boy® Advance

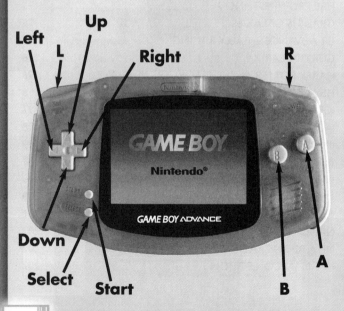

Left

L

Up

Right

R

Down

Select

Start

A

B

ALIENATORS: EVOLUTION CONTINUES

Passwords

Level	Password
2	MDKMZKCC

3	BHSZSKTC
4	ZKTSHKMC
5	JLPFDKHB
6	HMDBRKCB
7	GLDKLKZB
8	GLPKLKRB
9	GLDJBKKF
10	GLPJBKFF
11	GLDKBKZF
12	GLPKBKRF

13	GLDJLKHD

ATV QUAD POWER RACING

All ATVs and Tracks

Enter the following as a password: **Frog, Frog, Helmet, Speed Burst, Tire.**

BACKTRACK

All Weapons

During gameplay press SELECT, then press L, Right, B, L, R, Left. Now enter **WEAP** as a password.

Auto Ammo

During a game press SELECT, then press L, Right, B, L, R, Left. Now enter **AMMO** as a password.

Invincibility

During a game press SELECT, then press L, Right, B, L, R, Left. Now enter **GOD** as a password.

BATMAN: VENGEANCE

Passwords

Level	Password
2	GOTHAM

Level	Password
3	BATMAN
4	BRUCE
5	WAYNE
6	ROBIN
7	DRAKE
8	BULLOCK
9	GRAYSON
10	KYLE
11	BATARANG
12	GORDON
13	CATWOMAN
14	BATGIRL
15	ALFRED

Meanwhile, at the abondoned Gotham hemical Plant, the hide-out of Poison Ivy

BOXING FEVER

Passwords

Complete	Password
Amateur Series	90HG6738

Top Contender Series	H7649DH5
Pro Am Series	2GG48HD9
Professional Series	8G3D97B7
World Title	B3G58318

Complete	Password
Survival Mode	G51FF888

BRITNEY'S DANCE BEAT

Everything

Enter the password **HMNFK**.

CASTLEVANIA: CIRCLE OF THE MOON

Magician Mode

Complete the game. Then start a new game and enter **FIREBALL** as the name.

Fighter Mode

Complete the game in Magician mode. Then start a new game and enter **GRADIUS** as the name.

Shooter Mode

Complete the game in Fighter mode. Then start a new game and enter **CROSSBOW** as the name.

Thief Mode

Complete the game in Shooter mode. Then start a new game and enter **DAGGER** as the name.

CASTLEVANIA: HARMONY OF DISSONANCE

Maxim Kischine

Complete the game and enter **MAXIM** as a name.

No Magic

Complete the game and enter **NO MAGIC** as a name.

Hard Mode

Complete the game and enter **HARDGAME** as a name.

Boss Rush Mode

Complete the game.

Classic Simon in Boss Rush Mode

After unlocking Boss Rush mode, press the following at the Konami logo: Up, Up, Down, Down, Left, Right, Left, Right, B, A, Select.

CRUIS'N VELOCITY

Passwords

Level	Password
Pro Cup	HLDDRTSN

Velocity Cup	HLDDSNST
Velocity Cup	HLDDNRLN
Championship	HLDDHVGD

CT SPECIAL FORCES

Level Passwords

Level	Password
The Arid Desert	1608
The Hostile Jungle	2111
The Forbidden City	1705

Character Select Passwords

Enter the following passwords to select a character before the level.

Level	Password
Snow Covered Mountains, Level 1	0202
The Hostile Jungle	2704
The Forbidden City	0108

DARK ARENA

All Cheats

Enter **S_X_N** as a password. This cheat unlocks Map, Invincibility, All Weapons, All Keys, Unlimited Ammo, and Level Skip.

Invincibility

Enter **HLGNDSBR** as a password.

All Weapons

Enter **THRBLDNS** as a password.

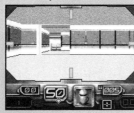

Unlimited Ammo

Enter **NDCRSDRT** as a password.

All Keys

Enter **KNGHTSFR** as a password.

Map

Enter **LMSPLLNG** as a password.

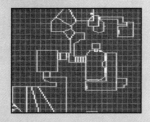

Level Skip

Enter **NFTRWLLH** as a password. Then pause the game, go to the map, and press SELECT to skip to the next level.

Sound Effects

Enter **CRSDR** as a password. At the Game Options screen, switch the Sound FX off and then back on to hear a random sound effect.

Passwords

Level	Easy	Medium	Hard
2	CRSDRPLS	VWHTSRGH	LDNHGHNT
3	TKMWTHYB	TCRSDRLR	DBYFTHND
4	TTLLSFRT	DFRLMWTH	CSSRCNHT
5	STCRSTRD	LLYRMGHT	HNSWLLSN
6	NTLVMLNW	WRMRCHNG	TSTRSTLR
7	NTTRDTNY	TLNDFRFR	STNDRDSW
8	RQSTMWTN	MHMNNCNS	LLRSCRSS
9	GTSTNDBY	YWHLLRTR	LNDTBTTL
10	YRSDTFGH	NFRCHRSN	SRCNHRDS
11	TWTHYVRS	DMSSKWLL	WFLLWRWR
12	THYRCLLN	TKRRVNGN	RRKNGNWR
13	GHVTBTHR	PGNFRMTF	DNTFGHTW
14	HLYLNDHS	STWCHRST	CRRYSGNF
15	TBFRFGHT	NSRCMNGW	CRSSWRLR
End	GDFGHTBL	THSWRDSH	DSFNGLND

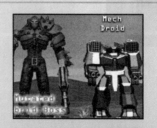

Game Boy® Advance

Cheat Mode

Enter **NRYRDDS** as a password. This enables you to enter the following passwords. Note that the previous passwords won't work.

Effect	Password
All Cheats	ALL
Invincibility	HEALTH
All Weapons	WEAPONS

Unlimited Ammo	AMMO
All Keys	KEYS
Map	MAPS

Level Skip	SKIP
Sound Effects	SFX TEST

Disable Cheat Mode	PWORD

Passwords

Use the following passwords in Cheat Mode.

Level	Easy	Normal	Hard
2	A	AA	AAA
3	B	BB	BBB
4	C	CC	CCC
5	D	DD	DDD
6	E	EE	EEE
7	F	FF	FFF
8	G	GG	GGG
9	H	HH	HHH
10	I	II	III
11	J	JJ	JJJ
12	K	KK	KKK
13	L	LL	LLL
14	M	MM	MMM
15	N	NN	NNN
End	O	OO	OOO

DESERT STRIKE ADVANCE

10 Lives

Enter **BS9JS27** as a password.

Level Passwords

Level	Password
2	3ZJMZT7
3	K32L82R
4	JR8P8M8
End	F9N5CJ8

DINOTOPIA

Level Select

At the Title screen press Up, Up, Down, Down, Left, Right, A, Left, Right, B, Start. Select Credits and allow them to finish to access the Level Select option.

DRAGON BALL Z: THE LEGACY OF GOKU

Invincibility

During the opening sequence, press Up, Down, Left, Right, B, A.

DRIVEN

All Cars and Tracks

Select Top Secret Cars and enter 29801.

Master Car

Select Top Secret Cars and enter 62972.

DUKE NUKEM ADVANCE

God Mode, Full Weapons, Infinite Ammo, and No Clipping

Pause the game, hold L, and press Left, Up, A, Up, Left, A, START, SELECT.

E.T.: THE EXTRA-TERRESTRIAL

Level Passwords

Level	Password
2	Up, Up, A, Down, Down, B, R, L
3	Left, Up, Right, Down, L, A, R, B
4	A, Left, B, Right, L, Up, R, Down
5	L, R, R, L, A, Up, B, Left
6	L, Left, R, Right, A, A, B, A
7	B, R, B, L, A, Up, B, Up
8	Up, Up, A, Down, Down, Left, A, B
9	Right, B, B, Left, Up, R, R, L
10	Left, Left, A, L, Right, Right, B, R

EXTREME GHOSTBUSTERS

Level Passwords

Level	Password
The Hall	HGBNL14VJ
Corridor	5PMDTF/K2
Office	21QSR9JTS
Big Building Boss	8G20S86SC
Racing 2	30J82JBMB
The Main Aisle	BNKN34SMW
The Crypt	V8JNNVGLC
Closer to the Underworld	MD*XN7KTJ
Racing 3	VD*PJKFTS
In the Wings	MDZ9KK/T8
Ethereal Ball	MD2TK4XTK
On Stage	WS0PJ6LTC
Broadway Star Theater Boss	VS31JL9TW
Racing 4	LDK9K6HTC
Don't Forget the Guide	WSJPJLZIV
Carnivorous and Hungry	WSFKP6WT3
The Final Confrontation	MS29P7JTW
Final Boss	VSFPPMHT8
End	LXK8KKFTL

FIRE PROWRESTLING 2

Select Talent Search from Manager of the Ring mode. Then select the following Fighting Style and Region to open each wrestler.

Wrestler	Fighting Style	Region
Dick Murdoch	Strong	America
D-Von and Bubba Ray Dudley	Any	America
Dynamite Kid	Showmen	Europe
Gary Albright	King Road	America
Goldberg	Strong	America
Great Muta	Lucha	Mexico
Hiroshi Tanahashi	Strong	Japan
Mike Modest	Showmen	America
Roland Bock	Stoic	Anywhere
Royce Gracie	Stoic	Anywhere
Salman Hashmikov	Strong	Europe
Stacy Kiebler	Showman	America
Tajiri	Showman	Mexico
Takehiro Murahama	Lucha	Japan
William Regal	Any	Europe

GRADIUS GALAXIES

All Weapons

Pause the game and press Up, Up, Down, Down, L, R, L, R, B, A.

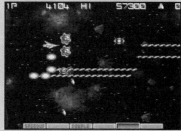

Fake Konami Code

Pause the game and press Up, Up, Down, Down, Left, Right, Left, Right, B, A. This unlocks all of the weapons. However, shortly after entering the code, your ship will be destroyed!

GT ADVANCE 2: RALLY RACING

Extra Modes

At the Title screen, hold B + L and press Down.

All Cars

At the Title screen, hold B + L and press Left.

All Tracks

At the Title screen, hold B + L and press Right.

All Tune-Ups

At the Title screen, hold B + L and press Up.

Credits

At the Title screen, hold B + L and press Up + B.

GUILTY GEAR X

Change Outfit

At the Character Select screen, press START or SELECT.

Fight as Dizzy or Testament

At the Title screen, press Down, Right, Right, Up, Start.

HARRY POTTER AND THE SORCERER'S STONE

10 Lives

During gameplay press SELECT, B, A, B, A, B, B, A, A.

HEY ARNOLD! THE MOVIE

Play as Helga

At the Map screen, press Up, Down, Right, Left, Left, Right, Down, Up, Select.

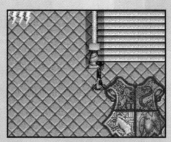

Level Passwords

Level	Password
1-2	mQJB0Cgxg
1-3	Vfcc#z>X-
1-4	&BtrYyly7
2-1	x6SMLJvcG
2-2	n5Gycvd5t
2-3	wfNGVylPs
2-4	ZN+!36QY.
3-1	Qw5YS6?pD
3-2	s:Ky2zd0t
3-3	+Xm<qB28l
3-4	5Kk9?r46B
4-1	>1WfSP%XN
4-2	m!sllSk+j
4-3	LjPK00GSf
4-4	4D87RI0MC
5-1	c1jnpQ%-N
5-2	w&xKCW>mv
5-3	7D8qYmM6C
5-4	fXc-bz1Sl

ICE AGE

Level Select

Enter **NTTTTT** as a password.

Art Gallery

Enter **MFKRPH** as a password.

Level Passwords

Level	Password
2	PBBQBB
3	QBCQBB
4	SBFQBB
5	DBKQBB
6	NBTQBB
7	PCTQBB
8	RFTQBB
9	CKTQBB
10	MTTQBB

JACKIE CHAN ADVENTURES: LEGEND OF THE DARK HAND

All Stages and Scrolls

At the Title screen hold R and press B, A, Left, Down, Up, Right or B, A, Up, Down, Left, Right.

JIMMY NEUTRON: BOY GENIUS

Level Passwords

Level	Easy	Hard
Asteroids	WM5DR5H3MCLB	2040YL61TT0T
Yokian Moon	KVZQG3Q50LZG	GGP6WCC273-3
Yolkus	51867F7MJ5YP	2H?-!L81TT0K
Yokian Palace	MMS-KXBVC4FS	+R6H!L91TT0F
Dungeon	N?+94T1?DJXW	456N$DWBWM?F

Poutra	939BSYT41N0Z	XZ16F2F8NS$!
King Goobot	BD5VVRDF3GXV	GRZB87HNYFR2
End	3L!VPH26V7$8	+CLT3LD1TTSF

KONAMI COLLECTOR'S SERIES: ARCADE ADVANCED

New Characters in Yie-Ar Kung Fu

At the Yie-Ar Kung Fu title screen press Up, Up, Down, Down, Left, Right, Left, Right, B, A, START.

> Congratulations! You have freed the parents from the clutches of the evil Yokians! Now you're one big happy family again. Good Job!

Improved Gyruss

At the Gyruss title screen press Up, Up, Down, Down, Left, Right, Left, Right, B, A, START.

Improved Frogger

At the Frogger title screen press Up, Up, Down, Down, Left, Right, Left, Right, B, A, START.

Improved Scramble

At the Scramble title screen press Up, Up, Down, Down, Left, Right, Left, Right, B, A, START.

Extra Lives in Rush N' Attack

At the Rush N' Attack title screen press Up, Up, Down, Down, Left, Right, Left, Right, B, A, START.

New Time Period in Time Pilot

At the Time Pilot title screen press Up, Up, Down, Down, Left, Right, Left, Right, B, A, START.

LILO AND STITCH

Level Passwords

Level	Password
Beach	Stitch, Stitch, Stitch, Stitch, Stitch, Stitch, Stitch
Mothership	UFO, Scrump, Stitch, Rocket, UFO, Stitch, UFO
Space Cruiser	Lilo, Rocket, Stitch, Rocket, Rocket, Scrump, Stitch
Junkyard Planet	UFO, Rocket, Stitch, Rocket, Rocket, Scrump, Stitch
Escape!	Stitch, Scrump, UFO, Gun, Rocket, Scrump, UFO
Rescue	Flower, Scrump, UFO, Gun, Gun, Gun, UFO
Final Challenge	Lilo, Pineapple, Flower, Pineapple, Gun, Gun, Stitch
End	Pineapple, Pineapple, Pineapple, Pineapple, Stitch, Stitch, Stitch

MEGA MAN BATTLE NETWORK 2

Hard Mode

Complete the game with five stars. Highlight New Game and press Left, Left, Right, Left, Right, Left, Right, Right. New Game turns orange when entered correctly. Start a new game, save, and restart.

MIDNIGHT CLUB: STREET RACING

All Cars

Enter **AGEM** as a password.

NYC Passwords

Character	Password
Emilio	NIML
Larry	GTBP
Keiko	LGKG
All (opens London)	LAPC

NANCY DREW: HAUNTED MANSION

Level Passwords

Level	Password
2	Ox, Horse, Tiger, Sheep
3	Rooster, Pig, Rabbit, Dragon
4	Rat, Dog, Monkey, Snake
5	Sheep, Tiger, Horse, Ox
6	Dragon, Rabbit, Pig, Rooster
7	Snake, Monkey, Dog, Rat

NICKTOONS RACING

Unlock Everything

At the Main menu hold R and press START, SELECT, L, SELECT, START.

PAC-MAN COLLECTION

Appendix for Pac-Attack

At the Main menu, select Pac-Attack. Then highlight Puzzle, hold Right, and press A.

Pac Attack Passwords

Level	Password
I	STR
2	HNM

Level	Password	Level	Password	Level	Password
3	KST	34	SMN	65	QTM
4	TRT	35	TGR	66	BRP
5	MYX	36	WKR	67	MRS
6	KHL	37	YYP	68	PPS
7	RTS	38	SLS	69	SWT
8	SKB	39	THD	70	WTM
9	HNT	40	RMN	71	FST
10	SRY	41	CNK	72	SLW
11	YSK	42	FRB	73	XWF
12	RCF	43	MLR	74	RGJ
13	HSM	44	FRP	75	SNC
14	PWW	45	SDB	76	BKP
15	MTN	46	BQJ	77	CRN
16	TKY	47	VSM	78	XNT
17	RGH	48	RDY	79	RNT
18	TNS	49	XPL	80	BSK
19	YKM	50	WLC	81	JWK
20	MWS	51	TMF	82	GSN
21	KTY	52	QNS	83	MMT
22	TYK	53	GWR	84	DNK
23	SMM	54	PLT	85	HPN
24	NFL	55	KRW	86	DCR
25	SRT	56	HRC	87	BNS
26	KKT	57	RPN	88	SDC
27	MDD	58	CNT	89	MRH
28	CWD	59	BTT	90	BTF
29	DRC	60	TMP	91	NSM
30	WHT	61	MNS	92	QYZ
31	FLT	62	SWD	93	KTT
32	SKM	63	LDM	94	FGS
33	QTN	64	YST	96	YLW
				97	PNN
				98	SPR
				99	CHB
				100	LST

PLANET MONSTERS

Level Passwords

Level	Password
2 England	H7Z3
3 Monaco	FDRO
4 Brazil	ZWWP
5 USA	SR8Q
6 Holland	GZW7
7 Japan	Z6FI
8 Kenya	KDC3

PLANET OF THE APES

Level Passwords

Level	Password
2	64N4HY
3	F5BMGF
4	BISKZR
5	76FNHB
6	P7GRXK
7	6B7VM#
8	QK6293
9	JDDUTJ
10	046PJ#
11	3#9QLS
12	CI2KYY

POCKY AND ROCKY

Expert Mode

At the Title screen press Up, Down, Right, Left, Left, Right, Down, Up, Select.

RAMPAGE PUZZLE ATTACK

Level Passwords

Level	Password
Tokyo 1-1	GQGGHKGBHF

Level	Password
Tokyo 1-2	LLMLMPLQMT
Tokyo 1-3	GJJBHKGBHF
Tokyo 1-4	BDFGCFBGCK
Tokyo 1-5	GSBBHKGBHF
Delhi 2-1	LPRQMPLQMT
Delhi 2-2	QKNLRTQLRP
Delhi 2-3	BFKGCFBGCK
Delhi 2-4	QBGLRTQLRP
Delhi 2-5	LQCQMPLQMT

Level	Password
Helsinki 3-1	GLSBHKGBHF
Helsinki 3-2	BGPGCFBGCK
Helsinki 3-3	GBLBHKGBHF
Helsinki 3-4	LQHQMPLQMT
Helsinki 3-5	QLDLRTQLRP
Paris 4-1	BKTGCFBGCK
Paris 4-2	LMLRMPLQMT
Paris 4-3	GJHCHKGBHF
Paris 4-4	BDDHCFBGCK
Paris 4-5	GSKCHKGBHF
Hollywood 5-1	LPQRMPLQMT

Level	Password
Hollywood 5-2	QKMMRTQLRP
Hollywood 5-3	BFJHCFBGCK
Hollywood 5-4	QBPMRTQLRP
Hollywood 5-5	LQBRMPLQMT
Washington D.C. 6-1	GLRCHKGBHF

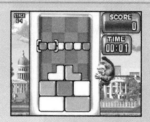

RAZOR FREESTYLE SCOOTER

Level Passwords

Enter the following passwords to start with the indicated level complete.

Level	Password
Aircraft Carrier	VDY3ZJ6LJVCQBF
Circus	ZBF4GJ5VJVCQBF
Construction Site	QHY4LJ2LHZCQBF
Scooter Park	SBY5VJ4BJVCQBF
Shopping Mall	QLY67J3BJVCQBF
Sports Stadium	7JY4GJZBJVCQBF

SCOOBY-DOO AND THE CYBER CHASE

Level Passwords

Level	Password
Coliseum	MXP#2VBL
Ocean Chase	CHBB5VBX
Prehistoric Jungle	5S@C7VB8

SPIDER-MAN: MYSTERIO'S MENACE

Passwords

W7HVI	Fluid Upgrade + Armor Upgrade + Hammerhead Down + Docks and Factory open

W7HZZ	As above + Web Compressor
W70ZZ	As above + Big Wheel Down + Chemcorp open
080ZG	As above + Left Wrist Container
Z70Zk	As above + Heavy Impact
Z787k	As above + Rhino Down + Museum open
ZV87k	As above + Scorpion Down + Right Wrist Container
ZV7Z2	As above + Fire Suit
ZV3Z0	As above + Electric suit
HV37k	As above + Electro down + Amusement Park open
JV37H	As above + Belt
JV310	As above + Symbiote Suit

JV31-   As above + Mysterio Defeated

SPORTS ILLUSTRATED FOR KIDS BASEBALL

All-Stars

Select Season, then choose Cheat Code from the Season menu. Enter the following codes to unlock these all-stars.

BAMSTAR   Riley Waters

BESTBUYSTR   Michael Quince

EBRULES   Nateo Geooni

GAMESTOP   Keith Fisher

GOCIRCUIT   Mark Modesto

SIKPOWER   Tecumseh Brown

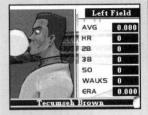

SIKSTAR   Eddie Penn

TARGETPLYR   George Stocks

SPORTS ILLUSTRATED FOR KIDS FOOTBALL

All-Stars

Select Season, then choose Cheat Code from the Season menu. Enter the following codes to unlock these all-stars.

BAMPLYR   Mac Marshall

BESTBUYPWR   Wayne Selby

CIRCUITFUN   Mark Haruf

EBPLAYER   Eddie Brown

RZONESTAR   Hal Church

SIKPOWER   Rob Lewis

SIKSTAR   Sandy Sanders

TARGETSTAR   Ryan Hunter

TOUCHDOWN   Sammy Rivera

SPY HUNTER

Arcade Mode

Enter **EDACRA** as a name.

Clear Arcade Scores

At Legal screen, press Up, Up, Down, L, R, L.

Clear All Cartridge

At Legal screen, press Left, Left, Right, Left, R, R.

SPYRO: SEASON OF FLAME

Blue Spyro

At the Title screen, press Up, Up, Up, Up, Down, Left, Right, Down, B.

Infinite Lives

At the Title screen, press Left, Right, Left, Right (x3), Up, Down, B.

STAR WARS: EPISODE 2 ATTACK OF THE CLONES

Level Passwords

Level	Apprentice	Padawan	Knight
2	BLDBGP	BHDBGJ	BJDGGM
3	BMFBHN	BHFBHJ	BJFGHM
4	BMGBDN	BHGBDJ	BJGGDM
5	BMHBFN	BHHBFJ	BJHGFM
6	BMKBCN	BGKBCK	BJKGCM
7	BMLBSN	BGLBSK	BJLGSM
8	BMMGTS	BGMBTK	BJMGTM
9	BMNGQS	BGNBQK	BJNGQM
10	BMPGRS	BGPBRK	BJPGRM
11	BLQGNT	BGQBNK	BGQGNP

STAR X

Unlimited Smart Bombs

Enter **GSBOOM** as a password.

Invincibility

Enter **GSHARD** as a password.

Full Weapons

Enter **GSMAX** as a password.

Level Passwords

Level	Password
Aquess, Part 2	IGIFCDLC
Aquess, Orbit	2EA3QD0I
Egaon, Part 1	NGK3QD0S
Egaon, Part 2	YGA5QSON
Egaon, Orbit	JGIXASPT
Birmen, Part 1	FECXEQ5I
Birmen, Part 2	ECMXUQXL
Birmen, Orbit	IIC3ADC0
Wolf X2, Part 1	ZLI3CQQB
Wolf X2, Part 2	MJC3CQAI
Wolf X2, Orbit	EJI3QDC4
Hades, Part1	BLCXQFVG
Hades, Part 2	YLMZAQVR
Hades, Orbit	2JAXABFQ
Tritopia, Part 1	MLI5ABES
Tritopia, Part 2	JTBFABRW
Tritopia, Orbit	QRLFADTM
SILICON, Part 1	NTBFABBW
Silicon, Part 2	MTLNAQAL
Silicon, Moon	ZSBPABEU

STUART LITTLE 2

Level Passwords

Level	Password	Level	Password
1	1377	4	6366
2	1487	5	6787
3	2278	6	5778
		7	5688

TEKKEN

Change Outfit

At the Character Select screen, press L, R, or START.

TONY HAWK'S PRO SKATER 2

Spider-Man

At the Main menu (or after pausing a game), hold R and press Up, Up, Down, Down, Left, Right, Left, Right, B, A, START.

Spider-Man Wall Crawl

At the Main menu (or after pausing a game), hold R and press Right, A, Down, B, A, START, Down, A, Right, Down. Perform a Wall Ride to make Spidey crawl up the wall. Be careful: This may lock up your GBA!

All Levels and Maximum Money

At the Main menu (or after pausing a game), hold R and press B, A, Left, Down, B, Left, Up, B, Up, Left, Left.

All Levels

At the Main menu (or after pausing a game), hold R and press A, START, A, Right, Up, Up, Down, Down, Up, Up, Down.

Replace Blood with Faces

At the Main menu, hold R and press START, A, Down, B, A, Left, Left, A, Down.

Zoom In and Out

Pause the game, hold R and press Left, A, START, A, Right, START, Right, Up, START.

All Cheats

At the Main menu (or after pausing a game), hold R and press B, A, Down, A, START, START, B, A, Right, B, Right, A, Up, Left. The cheats appear in the Options menu.

No Time Remaining

At the Main menu (or after pausing a game), hold R and press Left, Up, START, Up, Right.

Turn Off Blood

At the Main menu (or after pausing a game), hold R and press B, Left, Up, Down, Left, START, START. Re-enter the code to turn on the blood.

Jet Pack

Pause the game, hold R, and press Left, A, START, A, Right, Up, START. Hold B to fly, L and R to move left and right, and Up and Down to go forward and backward.

TUROK: EVOLUTION

Level Passwords

Level	Inventory Password	Level Password
1-2	K8T87 NL46K	6T8K
1-3	K8T87 NL46K	T7R3
1-4	K8T87 NL46K	4V2T
2-1	K8T87 NL46K	7NR1
2-2	K8977 N5408	VR0S
2-3	K8T77 NL42R	2T74
2-4	K8T77 NL42R	39KV
3-1	K8T77 NL42R	KV41
3-2	55987 L5452	V052
3-3	5K987 V5452	3678
3-4	5K987 V5452	LV15
4-1	5K987 V5452	3K21
4-2	5K987 V5452	9VL2
4-3	KK987 V2457	TV7L
4-4	KK987 V2457	5RTV
5-1	KK987 V245T	K69L

Level	Inventory Password	Level Password
5-2	KK987 V245T	759T
5-3	KL987 NT465	364V
5-4	KL987 NT465	TK8N

URBAN YETI

Unlock Everything

Select Continue and enter **TONYGOLD**.

WOLFENSTEIN 3D

God Mode

Pause the game, hold L + R, and press A, A, B, A (x5).

All Weapons, All Keys, Full Ammo, and Full Health

Pause the game, hold L + R, and press A, B, B, A (x5).

Level Skip

Pause the game, hold L + R, and press A, B, A, A, B, B, B, A.

Skip to Boss

Pause the game, hold L + R, and press A, B, A, A, B, B, A, A.

PLAYSTATION® 2

PLAYSTATION®

XBOX™

THE LORD OF THE RINGS: THE FELLOWSHIP OF THE RING © 2002 Universal Interactive.

MAT HOFFMAN'S PRO BMX 2 © 2002 Activision, Inc. and its affiliates. Published and distributed by Activision Publishing, Inc.

MAX PAYNE and the Max Payne logos are trademarks of Remedy Entertainment, Ltd. And 3D Realms Entertainment.

MIKE TYSON HEAVYWEIGHT BOXING © 2002 The Codemasters Software Company Limited. All rights reserved.

MLB SLUGFEST 20-03 © 2002 Midway Home Entertainment Inc. All rights reserved.

NASCAR THUNDER 2002 © 2001 Electronic Arts, Inc. All rights reserved.

NASCAR THUNDER 2003 © 2002 Electronic Arts, Inc. All rights reserved.

NFL BLITZ 20-03 © 2002 Midway Amusement Games. All rights reserved.

NFL FEVER 2003 © 2002 Microsoft Corporation. All rights reserved.

OUTLAW GOLF © 2002 Simon and Schuster.

PRISONER OF WAR © 2002 Codemasters Software Company Limited. All rights reserved.

RALLISPORT CHALLENGE © 2001-2002 Microsoft Corporstion. All rights reserved.

REDCARD SOCCER 20-03 © 2002 Midway Amusement Games. All rights reserved.

SOCCER SLAM © 2002 SEGA.

SPIDER-MAN and all related Marvel characters, TM & © 2002 Marvel Characters, Inc. Spider-Man, the movie © 2002 Columbia Pictures Industries, Inc. All rights reserved. Game Code © 2002 Activision, Inc. and its affiliates. Published and distributed by Activision Publishing, Inc.

SPLASHDOWN ©Infogrames.

SSX TRICKY© 2001 Electronic Arts Inc. All rights reserved.

STREET HOOPS © 2002 Activision, Inc. and its affiliates. Published and distributed by Activision Publishing, Inc.

TEST DRIVE © 2002 Infogrames, Inc. A subsidiary of Infogrames, S.A. All rights reserved.

TONY HAWK'S PRO SKATER 3 ©1999-2002 Activision, Inc. and its affiliates. Published and distributed by Activision Publishing, Inc.

TOTALED! © 2002 Majesco Inc.

TUROK: EVOLUTION © 2002 Acclaim Entertainment, Inc. All rights reserved.

STAR WARS: OBI-WAN © 2002 LucasArts Entertainment Company

GAMECUBE™

GameCube™ is a trademark of Nintendo of America. All rights reserved.

4X4 EVOLUTION 2 © 2001 Terminal Reality, Inc.

AGGRESSIVE INLINE © 2002 Acclaim Entertainment, Inc. All rights reserved.

BATMAN VENGEANCE © 2001 Ubi Soft Entertainment is a trademark of Ubi Soft Inc. Ubi Soft and the Ubi Soft Entertainment logo are registred trademarks of Ubi Soft Inc. All rights reserved. BATMAN and all related characters, names and indicia are trademarks of DC Comics © 2001.

BEACH SPIKERS © 2002 SEGA.

CEL DAMAGE © 2002 Electronic Arts, Inc. All rights reserved.

DRIVEN © 2002 BAM! Entertainment, Inc. All Rights Reserved.

FREEKSTYLE © 2002 Electronic Arts Inc. All rights reserved.

GAUNTLET: DARK LEGACY © 2002 Midway Home Entertainment Inc. All rights reserved.

JEREMY MCGRATH SUPERCROSS WORLD © 2002 Acclaim Entertainment, Inc. All rights reserved.

KELLY SLATER'S PRO SURFER © 2002 Activision, Inc. and its affiliates. Published and distributed by Activision Publishing, Inc.

LEGENDS OF WRESTLING © 2002 Acclaim Entertainment, Inc. All rights reserved.

MLB SLUGFEST 20-03 © 2002 Midway Home Entertainment Inc. All rights reserved.

MX SUPER FLY © 2002 THQ Inc.

NASCAR THUNDER 2003 © 2002 Electronic Arts, Inc. All rights reserved.

NBA STREET © 2002 Electronic Arts, Inc. All rights reserved.

NFL BLITZ 20-03 © 2002 Midway Amusement Games. All rights reserved.

REDCARD SOCCER 2003 © 2002 Midway Amusement Games. All rights reserved.

ROCKET POWER: BEACH BANDITS © 2002 THQ Inc. © 2002 Viacom International Inc. All rights reserved.

SCOOBY DOO: NIGHT OF 100 FRIGHTS © 2002 THQ Inc.

SMUGGLER'S RUN: WAR ZONES © 2002 Take Two Interactive Software, Inc. All rights reserved.

SOCCER SLAM © 2002 SEGA.

SPIDER-MAN and all related Marvel characters, TM & © 2002 Marvel Characters, Inc. Spider-Man, the movie © 2002 Columbia Pictures Industries, Inc. All rights reserved. Game Code © 2002 Activision, Inc. and its affiliates. Published and distributed by Activision Publishing, Inc.

SPYHUNTER © 2002 Midway Amusement Games, LLC. All rights reserved.

SSX TRICKY© 2002 Electronic Arts Inc. All rights reserved.

TONY HAWK'S PRO SKATER 3 © 1999-2001 Activision, Inc. and its affiliates. Published and distributed by Activision Publishing, Inc. Activision is a registered trademark and Activision O2, Tony Hawk's Pro Skater and Pro Skater are trademarks of Activision, Inc. and its affiliates. All rights reserved.

TOP GUN COMBAT ZONES © 2002 Published by Titus Software Corporation. All rights reserved.

TUROK: EVOLUTION © 2002 Acclaim Entertainment, Inc. All rights reserved.

XGII EXTREME G RACING © 2002 Acclaim Entertainment, Inc. All rights reserved.

GAME BOY® ADVANCE

Game Boy® Advance is a registered trademark of Nintendo of America Inc. All rights reserved.

Alienators: Evolution Continues TM 2001 DreamWorks L. L. C. © 2001 DreamWorks L. L. C. and DIC Entertainment L. P.

ATV: QUAD POWER RACING © 2002 Acclaim Entertainment, Inc. All rights reserved.

BACKTRACK © 2001 Telegames, Inc. Under License from JV Games, Inc.

BATMAN: VENGEANCE © 2001 Ubi Soft Entertainment.

BOXING FEVER is a trademark of Digital Fiction Inc. © 2001 Digital Fiction Inc. All rights reserved.

Britney's Dance Beat TM & © 2002 Britney Brands, Inc. Britney Spears used under exclusive license by THQ Inc. All rights reserved.

CASTLEVANIA: CIRCLE OF THE MOON © 1986, 2001 KONAMI & KCE Tokyo All Rights Reserved.

CASTLEVANIA: HARMONY OF DISSONANCE © 1986, 2002 KONAMI COMPUTER ENTERTAINMENT JAPAN. All rights reserved.

CRUIS'N VELOCITY © 1999, 2000, 2001 Midway/Nintendo. All rights reserved.

CT SPECIAL FORCES © 2002 L. S. P. All rights reserved.

DARK ARENA © 2001 Majesco Sales, Inc. All rights reserved.

DESERT STRIKE ADVANCE © 2002 Electronic Arts, Inc. All rights reserved.

DINOTOPIA © 2002 TDK Mediactive, Inc. All rights reserved.

Secret Codes 2003, Volume I

©2003 Pearson Education

All rights reserved, including the right of reproduction in whole or in part in any form.

BradyGAMES Publishing

An Imprint of Pearson Education
201 West 103rd Street
Indianapolis, Indiana 46290

BradyGAMES® is a registered trademark of Pearson Education, Inc.

ISBN: 0-7440-0206-0

Library of Congress Catalog No.: 2002113430

Printing Code: The rightmost double-digit number is the year of the book's printing; the rightmost single-digit number is the number of the book's printing. For example, 02-1 shows that the first printing of the book occurred in 2002.

05 04 03   4 3

Manufactured in the United States of America.

BradyGAMES Staff

Publisher	**DAVID WAYBRIGHT**
Editor-In-Chief	**H. LEIGH DAVIS**
Marketing Manager	**JANET ESHENOUR**
Creative Director	**ROBIN LASEK**
Licensing Manager	**MIKE DEGLER**
Assistant Marketing Manager	**SUSIE NIEMAN**

Credits

Title Manager	**TIM COX**
Screenshot Editor	**MICHAEL OWEN**
Book Designer	**KURT OWENS**
Production Designer	**CHARIS SANTILLIE**